DANCES OF TIME AND TENDERNESS

DANCES OF TIME AND TENDERNESS

Julian Carter

NIGHTBOAT BOOKS
NEW YORK

ISBN: 978-1-643-62234-7

Cover art by Julian Carter
Design and typesetting by Kit Schluter
Typeset in Plantin MT and Gill Sans

Cataloging-in-publication data is available
from the Library of Congress

Nightboat Books
New York
www.nightboat.org

CONTENTS

For Edward and Susan, who started it—

With Selby, who puzzled it through—

To Evan, who dances me on home.

Summoning

We stitch patterns with our feet.

Approach and avoidance, arrival and retreat. Hesitation, then a bold rush forward. Some nights there's an invisible circle on the floor. Tango dancers, who have a word for everything, call it the ronda. It rotates like the stars cast by nursery lanterns; galaxies go swirling by with the magic of staying up long, long after bedtime. But we're not here to watch.

Step into the circle. Your first time around, it's all you can do to keep track of your hands, your knees. Don't talk. Don't look down. Night after night. With practice, the world between us will expand. You'll stretch open to my warmth and weight, then past me to those others whose proximity gives meaning to before and behind. Each double body fills the opening that calls it in; each arrival makes an absence into which other bodies move. Occasionally people enchain, three or four transmitting up and down a line together, millipede. We feel their mass arriving and leaving. Our patterned supersession is like the chain of generations, except that we move counterclockwise against the flows of normal time.

A line is made of circles. Geometry is sensation. You can fall in love for three minutes. The music ends. We separate, find new partners, sit this one out, go home in order to return. It doesn't much matter who danced me when. Nights blur together, and nobody's taking notes or pictures: our hands are full.

Combine circles with lines, repeat the combination, and we've made ourselves a chain. Cast a spell, stitch a charm. We travel widdershins. Read this book as a charm bracelet come to life: linked arcs, partnered bodies, dangling stories, turning and turning in the round and shining dance. A circle made of bones and lightning.

AN OPENING, A CLASP

> I wonder if this is our most accessible way into history—not through
> grand narratives or identity politics, but through a simple one-to-one
> connection that we partially read and partially imagine.[1]
>
> —E.G. Crichton, *Matchmaking in the Archive:*
> *19 Conversations with the Dead and 3 Encounters with Ghosts*

Every chain starts with an encounter: one link joins another.

On the winter solstice I opened my email to find a cold call from lesbian
artist E.G. Crichton. She was starting a new show in her ongoing series
of queer archival matchmaking projects. This time she was pairing artists,
activists, and scholars with specific issues of *OUT/LOOK: The National
Lesbian and Gay Quarterly*, which she had helped found in San Francisco
in 1988. I was one of the 38 people she solicited to "dive into the *OUT/
LOOK* archive, think about queer history and use your matched magazine
issue as a score for creating something new and provocative."

E.G. gave me Issue #11, "Birth of a Queer Nation," from Winter 1991.
She couldn't have timed it better. I got her invitation just after Trump's
election set the whole world reeling. Things were bleak all over in the
winter of 2016, and that bleakness landed in my whitequeer transsexual
life like a whole graveyard full of ghosts.

A short list to set the scene:

⊙ 2016 replaced 2015 as the deadliest year for US trans people on
record, with 6 more Black trans women murdered than in 2015, and
we all know that record is always incomplete.

⊙ 2016 featured the deadliest event in the history of violence against
LGBT people in the US, which was a mass shooting at the Orlando
queer club called Pulse. 49 mostly Latinx people were murdered
while out dancing.

⊙ Police used fatal force against 916 US civilians.

⊙ Upper-income families held 75 times as much wealth as lower-
income families.

⊙ ER visits for opioid overdose rose 30% and 42,000 people died,
and honestly, I can understand just wanting to stop feeling.

I could go on but who wants to linger? If you weren't there, then, you aren't sorry you missed it. The point is that the winter of 2016 was the close of a trainwreck year and everyone I loved was feeling the weight of our collective vulnerability.

Flashback to 1991: the CDC announced that one million Americans were HIV+ and AIDS was the 3rd leading cause of death among people aged 25-44 years. Death rates for Latino and Black men were double and triple the rates among white men and the straight state was still in bed with the Catholic Church to let us all die and they still didn't give a shit because it wasn't happening to them, and a handful of celebrities started wearing red ribbons to advertise their earnest compassion for their gay friends who weren't junkies or whores or dark or poor, and nobody was even gathering data on trans people as such—and in all that ghastly mess, during my first year in graduate school, world-making trans historian and activist Lou Sullivan was one of the 29,840 people who died of AIDS-related causes in the US.

There is never peace without justice, and there will be grief as long as people keep on dying. Again and again, we learn: we can both mourn and organize. We can also throw legendary parties. I'm not hanging up my eyelashes just yet. Dancing was always part of this revolution and why shouldn't it be again, and still?

Through our actions the trans promise—
what we do with our bodies changes worlds.

If there's a theory in here, it's simple: things circle back around. We don't need all of time's wrinkles ironed smooth. It's pointless work anyway, because no starch survives a good night out.

My friend Susan is one of the mothers of trans history and theory. Back in 1991, though, she was an archives volunteer, busy transforming Lou Sullivan's paper trail into the Louis Graydon Sullivan collection at the GLBT Historical Society. Susan had just finished her doctorate in history, I was just beginning mine; but we met in a dungeon outside of time and language. The worlds emerging there were uncontainable. Oh, the explosive beauties, the resistant joys that flower in traumatized times: our bodies, our buildings, were molecules in a wild vortex, gathering and streaming and merging with others into fields of power, streets and coffeeshops and bookstores charged, all vibrating new worlds into being. We left footprints in memory, in concrete and fog all across San Francisco. In 2016, when I told Susan about E.G.'s invitation, I was fretting over the question: how could I bring that passionate movement forward? Writing didn't seem like it could hold us. She gave me a crooked smile to match her broken ankle, shrugged, and said *I dance on the page.*

She was saying *we always work with what we have.* I smiled back and said *I write on the dance floor.* I'd rather touch than theorize, but who's to say we have to choose? Back then I might have met you outside the modest purple Victorian on 14th St; presented you to my leather daddy Edward at the front door; ushered you into the dungeon with a sweeping arm as if to say *Behold our laboratory, our theater, our temple.* The venue's changed but energy's neither created nor destroyed. A body in motion tends to stay in motion, and there's no way to know what we'll find when we enter streets and buildings and bodies in the name of love. Transformative intimacy. Grip sliding and risk rising as sweat mingles, we can give ourselves over to pasts we shared and enter lineages we've never heard of. This is not a book, it's a series of swoons.

E.G.'s invitation was too good to turn down. Even before the manila envelope arrived, I was awash in memories of 1991. I unwrapped *OUT/LOOK* #11 with a thrill of recognition. I remembered this issue, cover and contents; I knew at least a dozen people quoted there. I spread the pages eager for a reunion kiss-in. But as I read, I cooled and shrank. Like the lights came on in the club and everyone else had already gone home: this object didn't recognize *me*.

It didn't seem possible. I remembered *OUT/LOOK* as a print utopia where activists and scholars and artists converged in the sexy-smart culture I shared and loved. I remembered Queer Nation as a gloriously polymorphous node where politics met cultural production met the leather underground. There were blocks in my part of the Mission where you couldn't swing a bookstore cat without hitting some kind of gender-naut. Surely some of that magnificent creativity was still present here? I flipped through the pages again, reread the article about the difference between lesbian sex and gay sex, and the one about the jack-off club. Table of contents, contributor . . . nothing looked back at me. I turned it backside front to read it in reverse and only then realized I'd imagined the recognition I'd thought we'd shared.

A CHARM, A POINTER

Each index is a time
machine. It sets
coordinates, sends us
point to point, shuttling dog-ear to ribbon
to finger, half-forgotten,
holding a moment wedged
half-closed, half-opening
to the spine.

Each index says
link here
and here.
Lined up in lists,
words wait
their turn because
they must;

we flip back and forward
and meaning happens in the space between

I put *OUT/LOOK* #11 on my nightstand to marinate while I attended to the politics of the present. I spent Trump's first hundred days in oscillation, turning toward the public in streets and airports, then turning in, toward home and kids and the question of what on earth I was going to make for E.G. One day I was walking to an anti-fascist protest when I saw a sign someone had put in a window: NEVER AGAIN IS NOW. It was written in thick Sharpie on a bright pink background like the Queer Nation stickers we used to make back in the *OUT/LOOK* days. A penny dropped, mine. Yes, I thought. That's right. That's where I'll start.

I stayed up till dawn stenciling Never Again is Now t-shirts, black paint on my hands slick and viscous like an oil spill, or the memory of state violence. Queer Nation had brought itself into being in the summer of 1990 when already 120,000 people had died of AIDS in the US and there was no sign that the epidemic had peaked or that anyone but us cared. By that time ACT UP was intervening in government policy and exposing all the ways the state was in bed with insurance lobbyists, pharmaceutical giants, and the Catholic Church; I wasn't surprised when my friends in ACT UP dismissed Queer Nation's relatively small-scale cultural interventions as superficial, even frivolous, responses to the emergency. It's true, we weren't organized for policy change and we didn't call meetings with the men in the suits. But that was the point. We were enacting different strategies toward the shared goal of a nation that recognized and valued queer life. ACT UP directly challenged national power structures; Queer Nation claimed queerness as itself a kind of sovereignty, our presence already integrated into the fabric of the everyday. We targeted the micro-political, multi-issue, and mundane. We showed up at pro-choice and anti-war rallies, protested police brutality and the first Gulf War, staged kiss-ins at tourist sites and shopping malls. And everywhere we went we advertised our presence with bright neon Queer Nation stickers.

There were hundreds of them, cheaply made in copy shops by anyone ready to put in the work. We slapped them on street signs and buildings and wore them on our leather jackets to advertise the intersection of our politics and our sexuality. The one on the cover of *OUT/LOOK* #11 said VISIBLY QUEER. Others said things like FUCK YOUR GENDER and ASSIMILATE MY FIST and DISEASED PARIAH.

Those stickers framed our bodies as protest signs and served as visual pheromones to attract like-minded queers. Our every movement was a critical intervention in public space. I wanted to bring that performance of solidarity and resistance forward.

Past and present keep overlapping. It is unnerving, not to say tragic, how many slogans I could recycle intact from 1991: PEOPLE OVER PROFITS; AIDS IS NOT OVER; HEALTH CARE IS A HUMAN RIGHT. Newer ones address newly desperate situations: NO KIDS IN CAGES, NO BODY IS DISPOSABLE, REFUSE FASCISM. I gave the stickers away at rallies and protests. They traveled around the US, to Canada, to London and Berlin and Sydney. I made t-shirts and phone calls and affinity groups. I summoned artists and academics and activists in coalition, just as E.G. and the other editors of *OUT/LOOK* had done back in the day.

And I tracked down the Queer Nationals who had been interviewed in *OUT/LOOK* #11. Miraculously all but one is still alive as of this writing. We'd never have imagined our survival back in 1991, when the obituary list in the Bay Area Reporter—San Francisco's fagrag of record—was growing week by week. Now, over 30 years later, those Queer Nation veterans are well-respected world-builders in their varied contexts: a public health official, an AIDS nurse, a middle-school counselor, an antiquarian and archivist, a lawyer, three performers, a novelist. . . Most of the dykes in that crew were still around SF. I got in touch. They couldn't quite place me, in the way that follows transition, so they weren't sure what to do with some strange friendly fag who acted like he knew them. But political action was urgent in that spring of 2017, and I organized good rallies. Everyone still likes free stickers. The Queer Nation dykes recognized the scent of my activism from our shared youth; I recognized their recognition when the air relaxed against my skin and they started sharing my cell number with their friends.

I never did explain how I knew them when they didn't know they knew me. I'd prioritized political affinity on purpose. You don't (I don't) build a movement by putting your ego on the front line; but my best efforts to bring *OUT/LOOK* #11 into the present kept reproducing my own trans marginality. That wasn't a part of the '90s I missed or wanted to bring forward.

I called Susan to tell her my time machine was caught in an invisibility vortex. She said dryly there was a reason she'd helped to found Transgender Nation back in the day: the queer nation alone has never been big enough to hold us.

Twin rivers flow through me. They carved the eager channels of my identification with the queer nationals and they flooded me with that old dysphoric loneliness when I could not find myself in the pages of the magazine. Each time my time machine/political performance stalled out, I felt my muscles bracing in the tide of my impulse to correct *OUT/LOOK*'s omissions and claim my place in the documentary record. Perhaps my old gay and lesbian movements should take a turn around the transsexual dancefloor. I could come out, assert my presence: for sure that's what my students would want me to do. They value disclosure as a sign of integrity and an affirmation of trans presence in the world. Their drive toward recognition speaks to my own and yet—I also understand my, our, illegibility as historically and psychically appropriate. Writing me and my kind into the historical record requires honoring aspects of trans/historical experience that evade documentation, and for which truthfulness is never simple.

It's not that we trans people are inherently deceptive. We were pushed. During the second half of the twentieth century, medical and psychiatric and legal professionals built tall walls to funnel wild trans potential into a very narrow range of possible expressions, all conforming to white middle-class ideals. If you didn't tell the doctors and psychologists stories about your yearning to be oh so normal, they could and did block your access to medical transition technologies.

When I moved to SF in 1989 that regime was just beginning to shift. Over the next few years, as hormones and surgery became more available to more queer peoples, a raft of my peers headed directly to the clinics. A few I knew transitioned into nondisclosing normativity as fast as ever they could. Others, like Susan, began to solidify trans presence in scholarly and political arenas. Still others immersed ourselves in a cultural aesthetic of shimmering indeterminacies, in cinema theorist Eliza Steinbock's lovely turn of phrase.[2] Maybe we were dabbling in black-market hormones, maybe trying to avoid being diagnosed, maybe just broke or busy working out original paths toward the beings we wanted to become. Some of us did our level best to become illegible according to the existing rules. I for one was ambivalent about becoming recognizable as Man or Woman. I had nothing to disclose; my nascent transness aimed at excavating the materials of sex and embodying them in new and changing ways.

By the time you document my presence I'll have moved on. Come out, come out, wherever you are, but don't look directly at me or I will disappear. Shapeshifter. Try checking your peripheral vision. I've never been what you'd call closeted, and I've polished the skill of hiding in plain sight. I splice the gay liberationist imperative to come out with the venerable trans interrogative: who needs to know?

A CHARM: Shelter

Recognition is a high bar like
a pike across the road. Hurtle over,
limbo down—

They say it is a basic human need, like
shelters, which
have rules called *men* and *women*;
no animals or sex, no dancing friends:
no shelter this, that can't survive
the means of my survival: no, recognition
is not always what we're after
or before.

Must I give
myself a name? Do you need to see my face
to know I'm real? I'd rather share
the motive force of change.
Spin me, Daddy. Our strong wrists crossed
and clasping, you redirect my energies,
you bring me in to let me out again.

Recognition implies that the me you can encounter now is the same as the one you encountered then but it just ain't so. One definition of history is *change over time*. One definition of art is *representation*, re-presenting. We do both when we're dancing. When I say I'm a social choreographer I mean I've had some practice reassembling bodies and spaces into recognizable new forms without ever letting go.

That's why this work encircles trans activist Lou Sullivan but isn't centrally about him—he wasn't my type, nor I his, and anyway he was already sick when I first came to San Francisco, and we didn't move through the city along the same paths. He didn't dance or organize rallies, and if he ever played at the 14th St dungeon, he didn't write about it in the famous Diaries where he documented his transition, activism, eroticism. Our connection is indirect. Nobody who moves with me ever met the guy. But we are linked by the carnal love you can find threaded through queer and trans archives—in particular through the archive presently known as the GLBT Historical Society Archive and Museum here in San Francisco, where Lou deposited his papers, where my young friends Zach and Ellis co-edited his diaries for publication, where Susan and I volunteered in different decades, where E.G. was artist-in-residence, where Queer Nation ephemera is preserved and my pink and black Never Again is Now t-shirt is housed. What brings Lou into this meditation is his participation in a history written in desiring flesh.

Back in 1985, before B and T got on the guest list for the LGBTQ-etc. acronym party, Lou was a founding member of the Gay and Lesbian Historical Society. At the end of his life he knew that his Diaries were important historical documents and he made some gestures toward editing them for publication. But when Lou had to choose between making himself legible for future researchers and keeping the memory of his own dead loves alive, he gave his last strength to his biography of Jack Bee Garland, the late nineteenth century sailorman who lived and died in and around San Francisco Bay, and whom Lou claimed as his transcestor.

> These past two days I read the entire text aloud, while proofreading it, and even now, five years after I began researching the story, it moves me deeply. I can almost feel Garland reaching forth from the netherworld and embracing me.[3]
> —*We Both Laughed in Pleasure: The Selected Diaries of Lou Sullivan, 1961-1991*

History makes the special kind of bond between people who met at a funeral. There is a transhistorical community of people who tend the same graves; strangers bearing flowers have been your kindred all along.

A CHARM: Winter 1973

For my sixth birthday my mother covered a small, fat blank book in red bandanna-print corduroy and gave me my first journal. On the flyleaf she wrote a dedication:

> *You become a writer by writing*
> > *a lover by loving,*
> > *a dancer by dancing.*
> *How do you become a supper or a sneaker?*

Mama, I figured it out! You find the right kitchen, and the right feet to wrap yourself around.

Transfer and transmission are complicated and vibrant. Our bodies have their own relationship to evidence. Eyes receive light as information; skin handles electrical knowledge; cities and fashions store memory in their own textured ways, and imagination has its place too. What archive are we engaging when I come eager toward you with my leather jacket open? When we hug we lean into an earlier way of being sexy, of living gender. It's stored in the sensual contrast between fog-chilled hide and the human warmth rising from within; if you were there, then, you might recall that thrill; but here and now that embrace would be a re-enactment, not least because these days we'd both be wearing hoodies. Sometimes transmission is a question of style. It's my job to edit and compose the past. What you feel through me won't be the same as it was, is now, or will be, but that's part of the point and anyway nothing is the first time twice. What remains consistent is that I am not a reliably reliable narrator (you've been warned).

I decided I'd done my *OUT/LOOK* assignment. I'd made my stickers and political performances. Minor work, I thought, but sufficient. I wasn't going to embarrass myself or let E.G. down. Yet I ached with the memory of the joy, the boldness of that past movement springing lively in my body, connected, the dance emerging between us in streets and bars, coffeehouses and dungeons. I could not let that vital rush die with me. Something remained undone and still, the magazine sat stolid by my bed. Clearly I wasn't its story to tell.

Then one night I dreamed I saw my middle-aged self romping hand in hand with a trans boy young enough to be my son. We were off to visit his lesbian grandmother. This still seemed like a good idea the next morning, so I made it happen and called it the Transgenderational Touch Project. For 3 months I forged connections between beloved young transsexuals and dear old queers, the dykes and fags and kinksters who were the big kids in town in 1991, when Lou Sullivan died and *OUT/LOOK* and Queer Nation and Susan and I were all hot young things in cool scenes.

Reader, follow me into relationships and dreams that happened then and next and before and in a few alternative chronologies, looping and crossing as they wind to and from early 1990s San Francisco. Some take place in those plague years, some take us back before history begins. I'm offering an alternative way to think about lineage and recognition by describing how historical kinship works, how it feels in all its looping complexity. Consider me a case study. I'm kin to Lou Sullivan through people I love and who love him as kin: Susan who mothered me through transition; Zach, beloved boy now grown; Susan who carved and curated Lou's remains and set him on his way; Zach who edited the Diaries, repeating her gesture decades later. Through them Lou's lineage twines into my own, and I am passing it on, passing it down, mouth to mouth and memory to memory.

But none of them—not Lou, not Susan, not Zach—took first form in dyke worlds. None of them began with poetry and motion. And I did, I did.

FIRST LINK:
A history of sexual charge

Like lightning, [imagination] entails a process involving electrical potential
buildup and flows of charged particles: neurons transmitting electrochemical
signals across synaptic gaps and through ion channels that spark
awareness in our brains.[4]

—Karen Barad, *"Transmaterialities: Trans*/Matter/Realities"*

I met Edward at the Catacombs on Shotwell Street near 17th—I can
never remember the exact address or which event—maybe my very first
play party, maybe an Outcasts orientation for newcomers to the San
Francisco leatherdyke scene? Either way it was mid-June 1989 and my
first weekend in town. Someone introduced me to the lone assigned-
male-at-birth person there. Tall willowy blond, he flirted fairy-in-distress
and within minutes he had engaged my services as a safety monitor for
Dykes on Bikes, leading the 20th anniversary Gay Pride parade.

Welcome to San Francisco. Edward was tactful about it later, suggested
that perhaps his interest wasn't only because he was absolutely desperate
for volunteers to put the parade on the street in compliance with its
permits; that perhaps he approached me because he saw something in me
that told him I could pull it off. Perhaps that isn't 20/20 hindsight. What
matters more is that right from the beginning I found myself responding
to a community's call to become something I'd never dreamed of, and
yet already was.

Back in those days my leather shoulder blushed purple with the bandanna that announced my taste for piercing. Red and blue and black and green: whichever flag you fly, whatever codes you use, you too exist in a condition of constantly calibrated opening. Permeability is how we're made, through and through. We have it on good authority. From the *Encyclopédie ou Dictionnaire raisonné des sciences, des arts et des métiers* (Paris, 1765), volume 12, page 215:

> One must cut a piece of the exterior skin, as thin as possible, with a
> well-sharpened razor; immediately after, you will cut from the same
> place a second piece that you put under a microscope; and . . . one
> will see with pleasure, light through the pores.[5]

Razorblades and light. I'll happily shear some skin to let these stories through. They're partly mine, and mostly true.

This is not an autobiography, it's an analysis of power.

I entered the dungeon when San Francisco was crackling with dangerous desires. Almost a decade into the epidemic, the structures of capital and state power were at best indifferent to our lives and deaths—not that they had ever given a patriarchal rat's ass about women's sexual integrity or survival anyway. We tapped into the circuits flowing with gay power and feminist rage. We didn't freeze, we firmed ourselves against attack. We didn't flee the battle, we turned to one another; at least, we tried. But we fought on so many fronts we couldn't always tell who the enemy was, what to keep out and who to let in.

> A cell's membrane keeps many things either inside or outside, but it contains channels that selectively let some material through.[6]
> —Peter Godfrey-Smith, *Metazoa*

Being porous can be dangerous. All sex is social and our own interiors were such risky spaces. Any of us might carry plague in our blood or violence in our fantasies, and anyway we knew the feds infiltrated every radical organization. We polarized over strategy. The respecto-gays and the pre-TERF radical lesbian-feminists said we should tighten our assholes, close the baths, deprioritize orgasm in the name of sisterhood, grow up and get married, stop doing drag, kick out the butches and the trans women, exile leatherdykes from the lesbian nation. Perverts like me said no, we needed to invent new techniques of pleasure, distribute desire over every possible surface of our bodies and our cultures, just be done compromising with those who hated us. It came down to normativity or latex—barriers against sex or sex with a barrier. We all wanted to find ways to make opening feel safe.

> Channels may have arisen initially just to enable cells to adjust their overall charge in relation to the outside—tuning as well as taming their charge.[7]

Sexual politics had been a cultural lightning rod for all two decades of my little perv life. No surprise, then, that back in 1989 I couldn't begin

24

to imagine a community that allowed for permeability. And in hindsight, it's no surprise that this was the moment when Edward founded the pansexual play parties he called LINKS.

Charged particles can set new events in the cell in motion. [8]

Those parties, those particles—oh the movement—

Edward started LINKS with an educated guess that he wasn't the only charged particle yearning to connect across boundaries of gender and desire. He was right. At any given LINKS party you might encounter leatherdykes from the Outcasts, pagans like the Radical Faeries and the regulars from Queen of Heaven, South of Market leathermen, kinky het couples from the Society of Janus, the occasional handballer or drag queen or rubber fetishist, lesbians with fantasies, rafts of transsexuals in the making, shoals of sexual adventurers. What we had in common— what drew us there and kept us coming back—was that we were sick of clamping down on ourselves and one another for fear of contagion. We were willing to risk opening to the erotic energy of the many ways we lived, to the plurality we were beginning to name as our collective queerness.

There is a reason that the channels in our cell membranes both open and close in response to electrical current, chemistry, and physical impact. We had rules to keep ourselves and one another safe: don't play high, don't chat in the dungeon, don't fuck without latex, don't bleed or pee outside the tiny back bathroom reserved for these things, and don't intrude on someone else's scene. Basically, as long as you weren't being a jerk or a vector you were welcome to do what you and partners wanted to. In that sense LINKS was not a political space—but in that cultural and epidemiological moment, our openness was itself a political stance. We sweated and shivered and absorbed one another's scenes. We spent hours parsing how our play refused and revised, reversed and displaced the larger pressures that demanded we comply where we would not consent.

It sounds so abstract now but then we were sharing the taste of latex. We were inventing new ways to share skin in the game.

Our bodies' boundaries are spangled with millions upon millions of portals at every scale. We open our nostril-gates and draw all sorts of crap into our lungs. We filter out particulates and water through regulatory channels, via increasingly delicate tissues until finally pure oxygen molecules diffuse down concentration gradients, along itty-bitty protein chains in our cell walls, and into our blood. Oxygen binds to hemoglobin molecules; blood carries oxygen all over us. Dutiful and promiscuous oxygen jumps ship wherever it hears a tissue calling breathlessly for its company. Left lonely, hemoglobin reacts by bonding with carbon dioxide that's been recently kicked out of mitochondria. Carbon dioxide goes along for the hemoglobin ride but that isn't any mammal's healthiest relationship, so the blood drops carbon dioxide off at the lungs, which then transmit the waste gas back through the many gated portals that connect and separate capillaries to your exhale. Air is released to make another set of bonding opportunities for oxygen.

Desire is a thriftstore treasure, used by you and new to me, recharged by its passage from hand to hand. My first scene with Edward worked exactly that way. He was behind in the preparations for Black Leather Wings' annual kinky Faerie Camp. This annoyed his leatherdyke top, who complained to my leatherdyke top, who then offered me as household service. At the time, I assumed I'd be carrying suitcases or some such but then Edward called to tell me to bring high heels to the date. I went a little blank, a little numb. That feeling of watching yourself from somewhere else. Want some dysphoric dissociation with that, dear? Sure, why not. I was used to drinking that brew and anyway I was too invested in butch cool to back out, so I went to the Goodwill on Haight and emerged with drop-dead vintage stilettos, fine black wool banded with a flat black matte satin ribbon, beautifully made and wickedly proportioned. They were the first really good shoes I ever owned. They're still in a box under the stairs, pointy toes bent and the wool worn through from crawling: their body, like mine, bears the material traces of more than a half-century's repeated pull down toward the floor.

> Voltage-gated ion channels are channels that open as a response to electrical events that they, the channels, are exposed to. This makes possible a chain reaction; a flow of current creates a greater flow of current.[9]

Seduction and response. Electricity doesn't disperse; it intensifies in its transfer.

> Action potential [is] a moving reaction of changes to the membrane of a cell, especially in our brains. … Positive ions flow into the cell at one point, affecting channels at adjacent points, which open and allow more ions to come in, and so on. A wave of electrical disruption travels along the membrane like a pulse. [10]

Edward was (is) much too crafty to force feminization on me. He simply recognized the disruptive potential in our adjacent charge. His Goth-femme self, Ms. Trash, spread out her trove of fairy-leather drag, selecting what she wanted me to pack for camp. Then she dressed me in her discards. Green water closed over my head. Everything wavered. I can still feel the twisting throb of the moment when I came up for air and found myself on my knees under their kitchen table, anchored to its leg by an electron transfer chain glittering around my waist. My membranes were plenty busy so I wasn't making much progress on the task at hand. Edward supplemented the chain around my waist with a delicate silver leash suspended from my septum ring. He said it was both decorative and useful and yes, it strongly encouraged me to keep my head down and concentrate on the work in front of me, no matter what else might have been going on.

I needed that metallic reinforcement. Too much electricity can fry your nervous system and silver is an excellent conductor, plus I hadn't yet learned how to tune my charge. Firing every whichway, I was still so young and (mostly) stone, so that meant I was butch, or supposed to be, and I didn't feel femme like the femmes I fucked felt femme, but they let me know I didn't feel butch to them, and the butches I wanted didn't take me seriously and girls were scary and straight men were dangerous and inevitably I was invisible to gay men and what the fuck, people, sexual recognition was something to defend against in shame at my own incoherence. But Trash grounded me. Lightning and gravity: it is remarkably difficult to raise your head when there's a chain through the ring in the end of your nose. She wrapped me in second-hand stockings made of channels. Gate after gate after gate I poured my ambiguity down the gradients of gender to land at Trash's feet, puddling around her fabulous shoes. And then she clipped my piercings to her own.

This is not an autobiography, it's a lab report.

> What we are witnessing is the potential face of lightning yet to be born—*a discontinuous exploration of different possible pathways*—before a lightning stroke explodes and shatters the darkness.[11]

There I was at the beginning of the 1990s, looking outward, chained and swaying in the current of my own paradoxical potential for trans femininity. Edward and I generated my first embodied transition together deep in the plushdark pleasures of the communal dragbag, where the abject blends with the beautiful and dysphoria converges with transformational change into something that, impossibly, already was.

I called Edward and told him that I was telling his story, only some of it was only kind of true, and how did he feel about becoming my fiction? He laughed and asked what I thought Orson Welles should have done. He meant in 1938 when CBS radio broadcast Welles's adaptation of H.G. Wells's classic horror story *War of the Worlds.* We're told that thousands of listeners panicked because they believed aliens had attacked New Jersey; we're told they misrecognized the boundaries between art and life.

> ~~Honesty? Accuracy? Tact?~~ These are the problems of all biographers, auto- or otherwise. ~~But the very broadness of the questions obscures the specific ways each can manifest itself."~~ [12]
> ~~—Samuel Delany, The Motion of Light in Water: Sex and Science Fiction Writing in the East Village~~

I regret to say this tale is apocryphal. Or maybe I don't. Who am I to draw the line between representation and the real? Words, world, bodies, cells, molecules—nothing about us is stable or entirely itself. Our skins are only the most visible of the boundaries with which we organize our matter and they, we, are made largely of gates that can snap abruptly shut or slip open; we are as easy in our being as the lace curtains that threw shadowmesh across Edward's bed, bringing sunlight and birdsong into the scene to remind me it's a vibrant breezy universe out there. Inhale, let go. A matter of scale. Molecular and microscopic mechanisms of transmission, intimate scenes of whole-animal transfer, we are entirely circulatory, entirely electrical, in constant shifting exchange with ourselves and our environment.

So, Edward and I agreed that maybe believing in fiction isn't the end of the world.

Throwing LINKS parties meant Edward and I ourselves rarely played at them but there were moments when we tapped into the collective current. One night in the kitchen I was dressed for work in combat boots, shoulder-length gloves, and the black tulle cloud of one of Trash's petticoats. There were people hanging around near the buffet, recharging after play or checking out their chemistry with someone new. How did they all come together in a circle? How did I come to be blindfolded on my knees at its center? I have no idea; what I recall is the startling sensory plunge. Edward gave me a movement prompt: *crawl to the feet that tap*. Laughter from up near the ceiling. A surge of uncertainty, and then the gentle percussion of shoes surrounding me. Tuning to the layered sound. At first it was like a rush of blood, too full for me to hear the heartbeats driving from behind. And then the rush resolved and I could parse each person's unique weight and rhythm so that I felt I knew to whom I crawled.

This isn't an autobiography, it's choreographic analysis.

Crawling is a transitive gesture. Like waving, like art, its meaning resides in the relationships it activates in its reception. When adult bipeds crawl, we often stimulate troubling histories of abjection. Our hold on humanity diminishes as we move like animals and children—creatures imagined as without reason, and subject to others' control. Artist William Pope.L has worked with these loaded legacies for decades. He is known for crawling in public, originally through the streets of Manhattan, later in other cities, as his reputation grew and people began to request him to crawl in their streets too. At first he wore a business suit to make his crawling body visible. The visual cue was necessary because vertical New Yorkers are used to overlooking poor Black men on the sidewalk; but a good suit in the gutter gets a second look.

> WILLIAM POPE.L: It's like Malcom X said:
> "What's a black man with a Ph.D.? A n*****."[13]

Predictably, the police with whom he interacted thought he was plumb crazy.

MARTHA WILSON: You crawled in the gutter to challenge the way black people are seen, and a black person sure enough took you at your word and almost kicked you in the face to express how upset he was with this image you had constructed. What was he seeing?

WILLIAM POPE.L: He thought I was degrading the image of black people. I wanted to get up when he said that; but then at the same time I thought to myself: Well, that's why you're here, that's why you're doing this—to offer, in a sense, an alternative he maybe doesn't want to see.[14]

To degrade an image is to subject it to forces that break it down. Acids and time act together; gradually the image fades. Eventually it speckles, becoming more or less unrecognizable. The paper that supports it may simply crumble away. An apt choice of words, then, to describe white supremacy's caustic and cumulative assaults on Black personhood. No surprise that Pope.L's interlocutor was revulsed by the spectacle of his brother in the gutter, nor that he expressed that revulsion with a physical threat. They were speaking the same language. One gesture replies to another. The guy who wanted to kick Pope.L in the face was, in a sense, right: the artist was embodying racial degradation.

Entering a movement tradition is a process of incorporating other people's prior physicalities. When we repeat their actions, we get a feel for their way of moving in the world and with one another; as we repeat our repetitions, we gain the fluency we need to pass that movement on. When we say that hurt people hurt people, we are expressing a similar temporal relationship to the embodiment of suffering. If we think of Pope.L as mobilizing a kind of dance technique, we can see why the man on the street was so angry: Pope.L's laborious, exhausting crawls intentionally and successfully re-enact the ongoing trauma of racial abuse, and in this sense, you could see his crawling as preserving—even promoting—racism as a viable social relation.

WILLIAM POPE.L: Most of the time, I feel caught in the headlights of contradiction. "This is uncomfortable. This is good," I say. My job is to negotiate these differences, and my art should suggest imaginative ways of negotiation without claims to complete reconciliation. Huh. That's where the magic be . . .[15]

31

Magic doesn't dissolve reality, it transforms it. Pope.L's magic crawls put the cultural trope "humiliated and helpless Black man" in scare quotes, drawing attention to its existence as, precisely, an image. You could say he creates an image of the image of degradation; or, better, he uses his body in performance as a vehicle for degrading the degrading image.

Equally, you could reject that attempt as an ugly failure.

Contradiction without resolution, power without control, connection without symmetry. Not everyone bears witness in the same way, and we don't have to articulate our testimonies in perfect harmony. Dissonance is powerful too.

But harmonious or not, crawling is a transitive gesture. I groveled in borrowed drag-queen lingerie to reframe the humiliation of having been womaned. Reframing, I rejected the punishing claim that effeminacy was a natural and pure reflection of a body called female. Pope.L's performance took a different object and moved in different spaces, but we share the crucial recognition that our movements are not ours alone. We shape one another's bodies in passionate collaborations organized by power's passage across our vulnerable flesh. Our gestures pierce us through with the sociopolitical conditions of their expression and the histories that made them what they are.

Permeability is risky as fuck. Consent is not enough. Reconciliation is never full. Energetic exchange involves relations of force as well as of flow. And still, some of us choose to reenact our abjections in order to dance them differently.

Forces, according to my high school physics teacher, are external agents—gravity, tension, drag—that change a body's state of rest or motion. In the abstract, forces are morally and affectively neutral. But nothing about them feels that way to this living body, this object whose mass is in motion, who lives its direction and amplitude in relation to others.

> By some mechanism that scientists have yet to fully explain, a storm cloud becomes extremely electrically polarized—electrons are stripped from the atoms that they were once attached to and gather at the lower part of the cloud closest to the earth, leaving the cloud with an overall negative charge. In response, the electrons that make up atoms of the earth's surface burrow into the ground to get farther away from the buildup of negative charges at the near edge of the cloud, leaving the earth's surface with an overall positive charge. In this way a strong electric field is set up between earth and cloud, and the yearning will not be satisfied without the buildup being discharged. The desire to find a conductive path joining the two becomes all-consuming.[16]

Perhaps the most beautiful piece of performance art I've ever seen is Julie Tolentino's durational duet *Honey (Cry of Love)*. Julie stands under a tall tripod, maybe 20 feet tall, her long neck arched backward to receive a steady stream of honey, pouring from the platform above her. She looks up along the line of gold. Her partner at the top of the platform looks down. Both are concentrating on the pulsing brightness that links and separates them in the changing effort-flow of their giving and receiving. My sweetheart Sleeperfreak leans over to whisper, *honeyflogging*. Yes. Hour after hour. Gallons upon gallons of honey run like tree sap in careful heavy drops of slow liquid filling her mouth which inevitably cannot hold it all. Sometimes she seems to be overflowing with sweetness. Sometimes it looks like she's being drowned. Sometimes she looks like a saint in ecstasy, or a medium possessed by some slow-moving spirit. Her face and throat and chest gleam, awash in translucent choreographies of dazzle, trust, submission, inexorable demands, luxury to the point of nausea.

What is it like to be her partner, Pigpen, perched on the tripod, overwhelming her in concert with her instructions? What is it like to be the tripod?

33

I brought the video to my undergraduates. I wanted them to engage with the creative challenges of how to communicate about communication, how to be clear about ambiguity and straightforward about ambivalence. I thought the lesson would be sweetened by aesthetic joy. I miscalculated: they winced and turned away. One said it felt like he imagined watching a rape would feel and others nodded. Well sure, I said, through my disappointment. This choreographer is indeed calling us to witness power's flow into and through her, and we can see the effort, the strain of receiving this other body. And what else is going on here? What shall we do with the artist's agency, or her insistence that this is a duet? What is the cry of love?

> Corporeal generosity, the giving between bodies, does not lead to
> two bodies which are positioned in the same way.[17]
> —Sara Ahmed, *Strange Encounters:*
> *Embodied Others in Post-Coloniality*

My students think that love wants safety. I hope my honey has the courage to know that risk is always on the menu.

One night I was digging around in the drag collection looking for inspiration and asked Edward how on earth Ms. Trash had gotten things so very dirty, and why she kept them if the grass stains wouldn't wash out. I was half-expecting another story about legendary queens dying young; instead, she got that predatory smile and told me a story about her leatherdyke top dosing her with LSD before taking her up to Buena Vista, above the Haight, for a late walk in the park. Like you'd take any other pet for a walk, except her ankles were tied together, so it was more of a crawl really, and their promenade was a famous cruising ground where men went for quick hot grappling in the overgrown shrubbery. Her top unclipped the leash, stepped behind a tree, faded into the fog. Silence, stillness, rustling. Maybe that was a footfall. A hand guided her head a while. Eventually: her top's familiar whistle nearby. Crawling through the underbrush, following the sound, her knees and the heels of her hands sank into damp earth scented with eucalyptus and bay.

Edward was cleaning his pipe as he talked. He carefully wiped the brass lid with the ball of his thumb, leaned over, smeared the schmutz across my cheekbone and jaw; looked down at me, enthralled in the nest I'd made of Ms. Trash's mud-stained lacy bits, and laughed in lazy triumphant recognition. Purred, *Isn't that a filthy boy. I think I'll keep it.* My spine whipped back like I'd touched a live wire. Thumb to skin, I felt the history of his sexuality penetrating my boundaries. His temporality and her tastes, unmistakably distinct from my own—yet also unmistakably alight in me.

Nobody knows how trauma is passed down, or what to do about it. Nobody knows how pleasure passes from body to body, or why it can transform the charge generated by pain. Mama taught me that fear is excitement without breath. Sleeperfreak says some people are turned on by the ambivalence they feel about their own desire. What I know is that I got both hard and wet under Edward's thumb, cracked open at the touch of a past that wasn't mine, awash in the sharp pleasure at the edge of violation. Oh, to be enough of a man to be that feminine on my knees in the San Francisco fog! But that story was over, the park long gentrified and I didn't belong in it anyway, and yet—

I've got you under my skin and back again. Intracellular fluid, fuckjuice and drool, honey, runoff in a storm drain; friction, glide, pressure, push, pull. We are awash and saturated by narratives much longer than our own lives, tales we can't control but must live anyway. They stain our membranes and sometimes the toxins leak through. And sometimes we can filter out the crap, metabolize those poisons toward euphoria. If we play safely we won't even have a hangover for the next century. We hope. But it's not like we have the option of staying out of history.

> One does not always stay intact. One may want to, or manage to for
> a while, but despite one's best efforts, one is undone, in the face of
> the other, by the touch, by the scent, by the feel, by the prospect of
> the touch, by the memory of the feel.[18]
> —Judith Butler, *Undoing Gender*

When we open ourselves, we can't always control what comes through. For sure we can't count on the dead to stay properly dead. They're notoriously indifferent, so we might as well quit fighting and become portals for their energy, with all its legacy of harm. It makes more sense to tune its charge than to try to halt its flow. Close the circuit, light up our haunted inner selves and maybe, maybe that's how we can heal the trancestors.

Once upon a time, there was a little fairy, on his knees in the woods, absorbed in private games. He was alone, but not invisible enough. There were boys nearby. Some will tear the wings off a butterfly out of spite. Some will push a pin through its thorax for the curdled angry pleasure of cruelty. They trapped the child before he could rise. They tried to bury him alive. He tunneled out and crawled home, spitting mad and filthy, with leaves in his golden hair.

Stumbling in vintage shoes, my face marked with ghostly thumbprints and oh such dirty knees: every time I've crawled into a gutter, I've both replayed and replaced the coercion he sustained before I was born, in a forest I've never seen, in a forcefield we share.

Whose lightning do you carry on your skin? Will you wear their stories tenderly?

SECOND LINK:
Of ropes and chains and sailing ships

Chains of love
Chain of command
Chain of fools:
a link on its own is not a chain.

It isn't even a link yet, only a loop carrying the potential for a linkage it cannot realize without company. A chain exists to the extent that it enacts the connection inherent in each unit's open structure. A flexible repetition.

> **Chain (n.)** A connected series of links (of metal or other material) passing through each other, or otherwise jointed together, so as to move on each other more or less freely, and thus form a strong but flexible ligament or string. Chains differ in structure according to the shape of their links and the mode in which these are united; also in material and size, in accordance with their purpose of fastening, restraint, traction, ornament, etc.

Move on and with me. Yank and bind. Freely constrained, our movement makes for strong connections through time-seas deep and green. Chains bind us now to then, and then again, and again and always before history began, and jointed with our pleasures now. Fastening, restraint, traction, ornament: it makes a difference what kind of chain we're in.

Fort Mason is located on a cove just inside the Golden Gate, crowned with a hill overlooking the Bay between the shore and Alcatraz. From time immemorial Ramaytush Ohlone people came and went until the Spanish fortified this point in 1797. Anglos pretty much left it alone until 1849, when California exploded with gold and the port of San Francisco became a channel for adventurers streaming in and money streaming out.

In 1851, such enormous quantities of gold were leaving California that the US military appropriated the land. The National Park Service pamphlet explains that the government needed to protect the shipping lanes "to ensure that the money reached its final destination. In an effort to protect what was now theirs . . . the U.S. Army established this overlook area as a United States military reservation." By 1912, you could stand behind the breastworks they built on the hill and look down on the sprawling complex of wharves, piers, and warehouses that supplied men and materiel for American imperial expansion into the Pacific. A million and a half men took ship there in 18 months during World War II. They are part of the story of how San Francisco became the gay mecca; but times and empires change, and by the time I moved to San Francisco, much of the bluff was comfortably neglected, the kind of place you could go to be alone with someone. Edward and I nibbled nasturtium and miner's lettuce as we roamed the embankment between the battery and the piers. Other times we clambered around on the old gun mounts. He told me stories about military technologies and tactics from Gaul to Iwo Jima while we looked down on the great troop ship moored below. Fog or sun, the gulls persist, and the creak and splash of the *SS Jeremiah O'Brien* rocking on her chains.

The metal links are enormous. Each is fully the length of my thigh, plugchunks of iron cast into flattened ovals and strengthened with a central bar (appropriately called the stud). Each end pierced through, like the holes lined up along the shell of my ear, but so strong, so massive: I fell in love at once. How could anything so heavy be so restless? The ship herself sings memories of prowess and pride, wrapped lace-beautiful in her rivets as she carved the sea to Normandy for D-Day. She's a floating document of Atlantic righteousness, Atlantic violence. Complex complicity riding high at anchor.

The Encyclopedia Britannica defines chains as "connecting devices," useful for "holding, pulling, hoisting, hauling, conveying, and transmitting power."

To approach, retreat, aggress, defend: people passing through each other's territories in the measured impassioned repetitions that define the history of nations.

Chains clipped to my septum ring, chains around my waist—

Since the Bronze Age sailors have used rocks on hempen rope to connect ship to seafloor. If you know how to recognize them, if you know where to look, you can find such anchors littering the Mediterranean's coastal shelves. Way, way back some of these rocks were lashed to branches to help them bite the bottom. As metalwork developed so did anchor structures that look like the tattoo flash of now, ink in a powerful bicep, pulling me down.

Chains aren't there to hold a vessel still. You can't really do that; water swells with wind and current. If you hold her tight, she'll sink. What you want to do instead: create drag and hindrance to keep her movement under control. When you drop a single anchor, the place it lodges becomes the center of a circle defined by the length of its cable; when you drop two, the ship swings between its moorings, suspended in the sweet spot where bound meets free.

To catch, bind, charm, join: compulsion meets desire.

enchain, v.
1. a. *transitive.* To put in or bind with chains; to chain up, fetter.
1756 T. Nugent *Grand Tour* IV. 73 The statue of Lewis [sic] XIV ..
with four slaves enchained, denotes his victories.

2. *figurative.* **a.** To 'fetter', restrain; to impede the free or natural action of.
1751 S. Johnson *Rambler* No. 159. ¶5 Bashfulness..may flush the cheek..and enchain the tongue.

b. To hold fast, rivet (the attention); to bind, attach (the emotions) closely to an object. Hence with personal object.
1844 A. B. Welby *Poems* (1867) 46 Thy song enchained a thousand hearts.

†**c.** *intransitive for reflexive.* To become closely united. *Obsolete.*

c1400 *Test. Love* (1560) ii. 285/2 Dignitie with honour, and reverence, causen harts to encheinen.[19]

I am attached
and riveted. Held fast.
Just can't break away from these chains
of love

In 54 BCE, when Julius Caesar invaded Gaul, he recorded his amazement that the Britons moored their ships with iron chains. How strange, he thought, that they had no rope strong enough. He left their failed technologies behind when he returned victorious to Rome, and anchor chains weren't reinvented for another 1900 years.[20]

Sleeperfreak, crocheting in the lamplight, looks over his glasses to ask me whether I'm also studying chain stitch. It's true: I'm seeing ropes and chains everywhere these days. He laughs when I say so and puts down his hook to bring my mouth to his. I let myself sink.

When we were first dating, Sleeperfreak bought 200 feet of unconditioned hemp cordage and entered into its substance, altering it with his meatstrong hands. He boiled it and burned it and bound its wayward ends with thread. That rope's long worn thin from its frictional glide across his palms, its own slithery body, and me. A dozen years later, one surviving length lies, sentimental, on the shelf at the top of the stairs into his bedroom. Its weathered silvery coil still murmurs *I can hold you.*

We both know I'll shrink inside its grasp so he cinches me tight as a packpony. The rope stretches in response. It grips the surface of my skin, melds its invisible cilia with mine, moves me timeless, invades me like a foreign shore.

> Prior to the introduction of powered capstans and windlasses everything had to be manhandled. The cables in the largest sailing warships were over 8 inches in diameter and the foretopmen, charged with their handling, were selected for their superior strength and agility.[21]
> **—John H. Harland, "The Transition from Hemp to Chain Cable: Innovations and Innovators" in *The Mariner's Mirror***

Strength meets agility: 8 inches across is two fists (no wonder boys ran away to sea).

> Following the Treaty of Tilsit in 1807, Napoleon imposed an embargo on the export of naval stores from Russia to Britain. [This explains] why there was heightened interest in alternatives to hemp at that particular juncture. . . . The advantages of chain could be

summarized as follows: first of all, its durability. Unlike hemp it was not susceptible to damage by repeated wetting and drying, exposure to the sun, or abrasion from a rocky bottom. Second, its ease of handling . . .[22]

It is a beautiful piece of historical luck that this vessel doesn't have to choose between rope and chain as technologies of connection. I like being easy to manhandle and at this point in my life I can safely say that whatever damage I've sustained has nothing to do with repeated wetting and drying. My interest is heightened by your willingness to navigate by the stars in my eyes. Oh, yes, hempen rope is hard to handle and why shouldn't it be? Its being preserves the material memory of being alive, seeking light, weaving wind.

A CHARM: Lesson plan

Zoom lesson plan and after-class notes from my MFA seminar on repetition, April 14, 2020

"Layered Histories: pandemic structures of feeling"
Guest artist: Midori (sculpture, installation, painting, social practice, performance)

Prep Before Class:
○ 10 strips of rag (canvas, paper—whatever's to hand) approx. 10" x ½" each
○ 1980s/1990s HIV art & activism (see Drive folder): Gregg Bordowitz in conversation with Douglas Crimp, *Journal of Public Health* essay on Gran Fury Art Collective, David Wojnarowicz's portrait of Peter Hujar
○ April 2020 COVID-19 journalism referring to HIV/AIDS: in Drive folder
○ NYT, "Early String Ties Us to Neanderthals" [23]

Questions for Discussion:
How does the past reappear in present memory? How do we string together past and present to make meaning? What role does affect play in this kind of historical layering or accumulation? How do we make, what do we make, in this moment's structures of feeling?

Notes:
What worked: Hujar portrait, questions, Neanderthals, rope-twisting workshop
What didn't: they don't know shit about AIDS/queer artivism
Next time: add demo for knotting or splicing all our ropes together into one

Technologies of binding speak from the deepest imaginable past. The first unmistakable fragment of twine in the archeological record could have been twisted as much as 52,000 years ago, millennia before Homo sapiens migrated into Europe. Its Neanderthal maker knew how to harvest and process fibers from an inner layer of conifer bark, spin them into string, and then twine three strings together in the reverse direction to increase strength and inhibit unraveling. 40,000 years ago, our species ancestors started carving bone into what seem to be tools for twining fiber into rope. I can see why. Twine can make baskets and structures, nets and snares, shelter and watercraft. It is useful stuff for people in motion.

What's knotted can come undone, what moves can flex. Binary gender may not have been invented until well after rope technology was in place. At least some archeological evidence points that way: most deposits of Neolithic human figurines include some that lack sexual features. Some paleoanthropologists argue that, even if these figures were implicitly understood as gendered in the context of their making, the absence of anatomical references suggests that "gender was not a simple, obvious binary system anchored in anatomy and obligatory to mark on all bodies . . . . Ambiguous figurines include examples from the Balkans . . . and Italy . . . that represent either erect phalli or a female with globular buttocks and a simple, shaft-like body. . . . In such examples, the gendered body is a freefloating anatomical diacritic that is applied to different contexts of action."[24]

I like the idea of floating freely, context to context. It's a relief to learn it took a while for Homo sapiens to tie ourselves down in gender systems that presume an immediate correlation between your basic biofacts and the way you move in the world. It's satisfying to imagine binary gender as a Bronze Age invention, as heavy as chain.

Long after basic metallurgy was a thing, people spent lifetimes refining
just one or two elements of the technique you need to make even the
crudest loop-in-loop chain, let alone the 3 millimeter links in the royal
tombs of the Fertile Crescent. Identical perfect circles, cast without joins
in molds made by blowing sand through hollow reeds, each tiny ring
filled with still tinier grains of gold and heated to the edge of melting.
Generations of mouths made nimble with time, inherited fingercraft
gradually building a lineage of goldsmiths who made diadems for early
Bronze Age royalty. Hand and eye and mouth.

You'd have watched a master, maybe, blow the bellows and prepare
the reeds and sand for carving. He must have led and corrected each
movement down to the pattern and intensity of your breathing. I
understand. I learned this mastery from Edward. I purse your lips with
my fingers and hold your nose. Here, put your hands on my sides, feel
the way I pull in the air before I slowly let it fill your lungs. The tip of
the reed obscures the cut you're making, so tune your ears to the sand's
sibilant meeting with the stone beneath. There is no chain that doesn't
demonstrate the connection it forges.

Corseted, bent over, holes open. Loop-in-loop chains are made by
pinching round links in the middle to make a waist, then folding the
waist over onto itself until the two loop ends approach one another. You
lengthen them by turning another pinched round sideways and threading
it through the previous link's loops, then turning it 90 degrees and folding
it onto itself. This open structure creates at least two possible attachment

47

points in each looping link: very strong, because made without welds, they are also highly accommodating.

Here, hang on to me.

Chain is smooth and chilly, decorative and implacable, quick to close around wrist or waist or throat. It's not like rope. Once fastened firm, it does not change in response to my deepening exhale or the blood that swells my skin. Extended under tension, it does not sing. It saves its commentary for a hard-tenor clatter when we're done and the links pile onto themselves between us, at your feet.

Chain can laugh—is infinitely extensible and dynamic—but it does not bargain or compromise or adapt itself. It simply is. Structure and substance, it is fully and only itself along its entire length, indifferent to my shifting senses. Whatever I do, however I imagine or respond to its touch, it weighs what it weighs. I am hypnotized and humbled in the face of its alien consistency, its contrast to my waves and tides; and anyway, I've always been a sucker for shiny things.

Homo sapiens have been migrating for at least 70,000 years and have worn jewelry for most of that time. We've had a minute to share our technical skill along with our DNA, our languages, our gods. Keep adding link after link after link until loop-in-loop flows like armies and markets along the Euphrates, the Nile, the Aegean. They are the golden footprints of people making contact, fighting and fucking, raising kids, laboring at trades, moving on. Sometimes they claimed one another's land, treasures, bodies. Sometimes they put their captives in chains, and sometimes they flaunted the jewelry they stole from those they conquered. Their ships got bigger but you can't bend iron like gold, so maritime technology grew towards one metal and jewelry towards the other, for a couple of thousand years.

Anchor chain, maritime chain, stud-link chain; different names for the same thing. You make them by bending hot metal bars into a coil like a giant bedspring. Then you cut the coil into open ovals, loop them together, force the ends toward one another, weld them shut. Finally, you weld a bar across the inner width of each link to stop the chain from kinking and to weigh your anchor down. For 200 years, those chains were hammer-forged. By 1815 the technological changes we call the Industrial Revolution simplified production and made stud chains much more widely available; Britain's Royal Navy adopted them in 1833 and by the middle of the century they were standard ground tackle.[27]

Millenia have passed since string first passed from hand to hand, cave to valley, as people who made art and wore jewelry migrated alongside herds of reindeer. Five thousand years since anchors were invented and golden link-in-link circulated around the Mediterranean; but it took until the early 19th century for technologies of gender, adornment, and seafaring to reconverge. My research for this book didn't include getting an anchor tattoo, or a return visit to the *Jeremiah O'Brien*. Instead, I stayed home and submerged myself in the cool sterling weight of an antique stud-chain necklace.

Not coiled and cut but cast in two parts which are then soldered together, this silver choker has slightly flared studs spreading each link so that each oval contains two circles. Its recursive complexity is hypnotizing. Each shining link reflects the shadow and light of its own body and the smooth round bales that join it to the others. So many curves, so many holes. Fondling and folding, my hands learn how the stud constricts the free play of the links so that they cannot kink. Somewhere I read that this is the essence of its maritime appeal. If you're a ship, the chains of an anchor must feel like the weights dancers sometimes wrap around their ankles; they keep you grounded, give you something against which to explore your range of motion. Translated into statement jewelry, anchor chain has less to say about fluidity and unexpected intersection than about the inexorability of dominance. Which is not so new.

> Chains are one of the most ancient devices for tying (fastening) and lifting, and their origin antedates reliable history. They were used by all ancient nations familiar with the art of working metals, and the oldest preserved representations of early life show their application for securing prisoners.[28]
> —Anonymous, THE IRON AGE, vol. LXX, July 3, 1902

What naval officer commissioned, bought, paid for this necklace? It sits low and close like a hand wrapped slowly round my throat, palm smooth, fingers and thumb unfurling to rest across vein and artery. This chain was designed to flaunt its wearer's status as a prized possession. Too bold for a courtship, too substantial for a dalliance: I imagine it was made for a wife. Style and scale date it around 1880. At this time, despite several decades of gradual reform in both the United States and the United Kingdom, married women did not have blanket or generalizable rights to own property, including their own persons. In 1869, five years after the 13th Amendment announced the formal end to chattel slavery in the United States, Harriet Beecher Stowe campaigned for the expansion of married women's rights:

> [T]he position of a married woman . . . is, in many respects, precisely similar to that of the negro slave. She can make no contract and hold no property; whatever she inherits or earns becomes at that moment the property of her husband. . . . Though he acquired a fortune through her, or though she earn a fortune through her talents, he is the sole master of it, and she cannot draw a penny. . . . [I]n the English common law a married woman is nothing at all. She passes out of legal existence.[29]
> —Melissa J. Homestead, *American Women Authors and Literary Property, 1822–1869*

Really, Harriet. There's a crucial difference between owning property and being property. Stowe was appealing to whiteness, summoning her audience to share her outrage that Anglo women were not properly distinguished from and elevated above the status of "the negro slave." You can't compare a sterling anchor-chain collar bestowed as a gift and the literal fetters imposed, by force, on enslaved people. Yet that contrast is so starkly meaningful because these objects do rhyme: in 1992, the artist Fred Wilson mined the collections of the Maryland Historical Society to bring such links to light, creating installations that combined and contrasted elegant carved furniture for a wealthy white drawing room with the brutal simplicity of a whipping post, the exuberant luxury of a silver repoussé table service with a pair of wrought iron shackles.[30]

Once upon a time, a man in a trim blue coat presented his white wife with a massive silver collar. Maybe he clasped it around her throat; maybe this was a parting gesture, an anchoring, that chained her to her place in their circle while he went off to command a warship's men and boys. All of this happened long before we were born.

We don't have the power to remove ourselves from history: the circling chains that set me sailing bind us to their ancient cargo: domination and adornment, hierarchy, suffering, skill.

A CHARM: Lesbian poetry

in the place where
her breasts come together
two thumbs' width of
channel ride my
eyes to anchor
hands to angle
in the place where
her legs come together
I said 'you smell like the
ocean' and lay down my tongue
beside the dark tooth edge
of sleeping
'swim' she told me and I
did, I did[31]

—Judy Grahn
San Francisco, 1971

A CHARM: Lineage

Genus Homo was aboriginally arboreal.

Maybe that's why when we think about family, we picture branches reaching up and back, down and across, each one of us a leaf, green growing tip or maybe an acorn dropping into another family's soil; but that's not how we live, not us sapiens and not our *neanderthalensis* cousins who looked at conifers and figured out how to make string. Families don't grow wild. Kinship is manufactured like rope and history and gender and trade routes and fine gold chain. Kinship is the stuff of the world we choose to hold precious. We wind through one another's links.

Catch, latch, curve; load bearing under tension is another way of saying *faithful*.

THIRD LINK:
Clarity, elegy, opacity

Cause of death: heart stopped. Well, yes. That's always true. Except for those whose hearts refract and scatter bright as the tears that fly when you drop a stone into a pool.

One August, Sleeperfreak and I drove out of Oakland at dawn to climb your ladder on a sunny LA afternoon. When we arrived, you were wrapped in ambient music and white linen. After the first flurry of kisses, you went back to writing and we peeled off our sweaty road clothes to spread ourselves out naked on the rug. Time passed. We breathed. Your fingers made tappity tap noises, keyboard like rain on the roof. Eventually you went to pee. Moving over our cooling limbs you looked down at us, rested your finger to the corner of your mouth—nodded—and said meditatively to yourself, I like this. This is good, that you arrive this way; and then your famous gurgling laugh.

Choreographer to my dancer, your flow shaped my solid rock. Dry stream.

During the plague years of the 1980s, artist Scott Burton stopped making gay performances to focus on what he called furniture sculpture.[32] He shaped big blocks of granite and marble into abstracted anthropomorphic forms and put them in public parks and promenades where men once went to cruise for sex. The flat backs of crawling men are translated into benches that invite you to sit on them; square polished chests stand tall for you to rest against. If you're not in on these sculptures' queer secrets you wouldn't stop to think about how the stones turn towards one another, turn toward the shrubberies. When they use this public sculpture, unsuspecting straight people reenact lost cultures of cruising. One after another they scoot their asses into frozen faggot laps; ghosts watch from the bushes, laughing til they cry.

How could you not have loved that work? Your performances of encounter also strolled the razor's edge between explicit and opaque. When I told you about Burton's furniture you invited me to recreate a performance sculpture you'd done with many others. Dancers came to watch you circle my chair, duct tape unspooling behind you in a silvery blur that traced the line of your slow deliberate touch. I gained legs, lost arms. You lowered my new body to the floor and invited the audience to interact. They touched what they pleased and curled themselves into the corners of my abstract anonymity.

Such a trans skill, this hiding in plain sight. Flagrant meets invisible. The subtle boldness of being what you are, doing what you do.

Not all art is easy to engage. Not all stories are true. I gather what words I can and send them stuttering along in the wake of the flesh. The best I can offer: your life broke and flashes in the mouth of mourning.

Far more people die during sex than you'd know from reading the obituaries.

Sleeperfreak tells me about disenfranchised grief. That's what it's called when we mourn harder than other people think we're entitled to. The dyke bar closes. Someone cuts down the fig tree. We are marginal to the public story of your Official Family, your public loves, and I can't even call you by name without things getting all political, so I'll call you what you called me—darling, darling, a name we share with a million others.

After our darling died Sleeperfreak and I went back to LA to join the other mourners. We lay on the studio floor and listened as dozens of mourners spoke of special intimacies, each personal, unique, and precious. Each tale was true. And yet our Darling's death left rings, concentric circles of information and ignorance, that allowed some stories to surface while others stayed submerged. I know enough to know that there is more to the story than their Partnerman and Mother will admit. I know enough that my silence is complicity in a lie.

We've been here before, I think in my bitterness. This falsity is like AIDS—then I catch the words before they're uttered. One loss is not a generation. Still the resonance is real. Mother and Partnerman colluded to hide and destroy the evidence of your expanding desire. They could not tolerate the reality that you died in a dungeon, happy, with another man. They put on the mantle of The Family and claimed they were protecting their Darling's reputation. Maybe they even believed that story. Mine is that The Family was willing to kill my Darling twice rather than acknowledge they died exactly as they moved: floodgates open to creative agency, surfaces rippling with joy.

Who am I to take their story back? Another mourner, intimate and informed, disenfranchised, confronting the limits of disclosure. Stepping into that river again.

We have continued to explore the edges of silence. One day it's sharp and bitter, a knife held between my lips. On other days it's a weight on the back of my tongue. We experiment with gags: ropes and ribbons, bandannas, pieces of wood and paper, bits of hardware. The psalms tell us the dead have mouths filled with dust. We learn that the living overflow. Gag after gag darkens with my saliva; silver trails spill down my chin, glisten in the hair on my chest. Holding back produces the leakage it seeks to avoid.

I document these scenes with drawings and hang them on a gallery wall. I want to show that mourning is a social thing, like gender and secrets.

Once upon a time, Sleeperfreak and I stood guard over our Darling, protecting and encouraging as their restlessness became unbearable and ambiguity was no longer enough. We shone on their shimmer, loaned our strength to their tide, loved them as they tumbled over their personal dam; but there's not yet a name for the sacred role they asked us to take on. At the end, they were not a gay man with their gay-man partner. They died in motion, wearing lace in someone else's arms. So here we are, holders of that most intimate and tender knowing, and yet lacking whatever certificate would guarantee our place at the graveside.

Sometimes I wear the white linen our Darling left behind the last time they came to visit. I practice their posture, turn my head, confront six ways it's not enough to re-enact their ripple. I want them to envelop me again. I want to feel their current moving me. I consider holding a séance to make sure they know they're welcome here if indeed they're still attached to living by some thread I can't sense. I don't know anything about mediumship, but I have been their medium. I am not ready to let go of being the mortal clay they molded for their art. Performance-substance. Dancer. Body.

From our collaboration notes:

"Allowing oneself to be seen in the process of doing"
"Performance as a vehicle for dealing with bereavement"

What is the performance of a bereavement that is in process? A loss that's ongoing, an event that is over, yet refuses to be located in time? How to summon our dead Darling's absence as an ongoing present thing, its substance inflected by layers of dishonesty about their life and the manner of its ending?

Every dance is made out of next steps. We all start out tentative, build our compositions out of uncertainty. We sharpen focus through repetition and variation. I take my Darling with me as I go to openings and performances, read, take potential collaborators to coffee. It's not that hard; the weight of absence doesn't need much space. Next to my Darling I was conscious of my relative meatiness. They wouldn't have chosen to be born into a body as solid as mine. And yet my Darling loved my physical presence, the shape and density of me, and the things those made possible. My form fit their aesthetic intentions.

One morning we were working together on the loft floor. Struck by their beauty I took a photograph of them. They replied with a photograph of me. Bold in their vision, in their pleasure and privileged access, the image dwells on the fullness of my muscles, mounded curves of calf and ass and shoulders rising and rolling away to the image horizon like California's coastal hills.

I suppose the picture testifies, in the usual indexical way, to the fact that we worked naked that morning. Its content and composition imply our easy intimacy in being bodies together. But its central work is its assertion of choreographic authority: our Darling saw the shapes I make in space and used these to create an image that differed from and exceeded me. I treasure that sense of not quite recognizing myself. It is a record of our Darling's unique relation to my properties as a visual and kinetic object, their documentation of a material that they might choose to deploy.

Roland Barthes wrote that photographs are spectral things that preserves the body against its inevitable future absence. Yet I'm still here, and our Darling is dead; and when I'm dead too, this image will continue to testify to their aesthetic vision.

So here I am, the stuff with which our Darling was making art. I'm available. Here I am, on the studio floor, still, again. I'm ready to be used. But there are technical difficulties. How to invite my Darling's occupation, how to loan them my flesh, when theirs is neither alive nor intact nor laid to rest? For five months the Coroner's Office prolonged the second that our Darling stopped breathing. Autopsies, toxicology reports, investigative questioning: these things follow from death in the dungeon, and yet they make any sense of finality impossible. Those darling bones and my grieving are suspended, together, in a tense that has no grammatical counterpart.

Our darling has died, as I will; and yet their death remains an open case. Open as in without resolution. Open like a screen door swinging in a hot drought wind.
Darling had a trick of opening their eyes very wide and blue

Earnest
Receptive
As though the pump of their breathing still powered my own
As though sensation were matter

As though the stories we made were still alive.

A CHARM: The Family (not vultures)

Once upon a time, our people died young and The Family swooped down to steal what remained. Some claimed their fear was love. Some didn't bother with the lies. I knew a man who swallowed hard and invited his lover's absentee sister to spread his ashes on Mt. Tam. He had wanted his body to feed the redwoods. The soaring trees look south across the Golden Gate where San Francisco rises from the water like Oz, or heaven. Sister didn't reply. But when the man got home that night the house was stripped: she'd used his absence as her chance to take every book, every pair of socks, every stick of furniture. Later, too numb to rage, he couldn't stop asking why she locked the door behind her.

But of course she turned that key. Warding off, shutting out, closing down the channels: it was never about protecting anyone, not even The Family and their illusions. The Family resented the hell out of our refusal to let them control our bodies. They would not forgive our unrepentant opening into worlds they did not control. The spread of throat and sphincter and heart, the yes of arching spine and clutching hand: we rejoiced in expansions they'd have denied if we'd let them.

They took their revenge.

Some families stole it all. Others simply stopped paying the rent and let the landlord throw everything out onto the sidewalk or into a dumpster and never came to get the body.

When you grieve, please don't malign the vultures that wheel above the mountain. *Cathartes aura.* Their name means cleansing wind, purifying breath. They come to clean the bones for us. They don't care how we died or that we find their appetites revolting. Queer birds wild and shameless they seek us out, take us in, absorb us, cherish and receive us as nourishment. We should salute them when they wheel overhead. I promise to lie down for them when it's my turn, to make it easy for the ones who come along to carry my bones.

FOURTH LINK:
Skip to my Lou

Once upon a time, people in Northern Europe and the British Isles used stone axes to split enormous oak trees in half. They laid out long chambers framed with forest and roofed with hills they built with bucketfuls of chalk and clay. They brought the newly dead inside to lie for a time, doing the things that corpses do in private. Then they returned to dance with them again.

> Where fully ordered skeletons occur within timber chambers,
> they are often located at one end of the [barrow] structure, with
> disarranged or stacked bones at the other. . . . The linear space of
> the chamber was a 'conduit' through which the corpse passed as it
> decayed and was dismembered.[33]
> **Paleoarcheologist Julian Thomas, *Death and
> the Body in Neolithic Britain***

Such barrows are places of enchantment and power. You enter the hill from a new car park marked with an apologetic sign explaining how the old car park had accidentally paved over a site of archeological significance. Once inside, dimmed spotlights guide you along the chain of low rooms over a boardwalk that protects the earth from your feet. These hills have stood for 5000 years, green ridges where the barrow-builders layered rock and bone and tree, but the grassy paths they made by walking are long gone.

Following herds, following seasons, how far did these ancient ones roam in a lifetime? How much further after they died?

A night's rest gets you ready for the next day's travel:

> The [burial] pattern appears to be one of complete bodies
> being introduced into the chamber and progressively becoming
> disaggregated . . . [in] a process of successive inhumation, with
> skeletal parts being carefully moved to the back of the chamber as
> they became defleshed.[34]

The barrow builders buried their people again and again, each time moving the dead along to the next stage of their underground migration. This must have required skillful collective choreography. First someone would have to do the work of opening the mound, lifting stones, shoveling away the worm-rich soil. You'd need a team of young strong backs. You'd need to hold your breath against the darkness. You'd need time and torchlight, steady heart and mind and hand to cut and carry rotting kin further, deeper under the hill. Was this women's work, midwifing the dead? Was encountering the ancestors like this a part of coming of age, or a shamanistic role for elders? It is hard to imagine it as mostly a matter of muscle, yet it must have been intensely physical work, maneuvering freshly dead weight along those narrow stone passages. If you didn't want to drag the corpse, you'd have to carry it slung across your back; you might bark your knuckles, bruise your shoulders.

Inhale the dead. So far, so grisly from one perspective, but it's what we do in archives: break down the remains to dispose of the nonessentials, then sort what's left with care. We make ancestors by curating their bones.

The barrow docent says reasonable things about national heritage and staying on the path.

Once upon a time, before I was born, an artist named Long walked a straight path across an English meadow and back again. The grass bent and parted where he passed. The resulting humble, elegant, and mysterious land sculpture survives in a photograph called *A Line Made by Walking*. Long's name goes under the picture on the gallery wall, but nothing in the image itself can tell us whose footsteps danced down that long soft channel to vanish in the trees, what comb parted the long hair ready for braiding behind each ear. Who was it, there in the grass? Long didn't start out as the body that had made a line by walking. Only in the act—through it, repeated, back and forth—did he become the body that had so moved. A body indubitable, impossible to anticipate, existing only in the past, and yet still present as a potential for a future in which someone, anyone, can walk repeatedly across a meadow.

This is not a memoir it's collective memory.
This is not about identity it's about history.

My ancient dead began to stir when juicy youngman Zach reached out to me with a question about the politics of queer community archives. At the time I was both flattered and amused that he was asking me for my perspective as a Real Historian (that never happens), so I picked him up outside San Francisco Main Library to carry him home. Winding through traffic I asked him what he was up to in the Lou Sullivan collection: editing the Diaries for publication, he said, but don't tell yet. The project's gotten all political.

Was it ever not? Everyone's got an opinion about where which bones belong. Everyone has to show their credentials at the archivist's desk. Like Charon, you trade your name for a chance to visit the dead. The ferryman gives it back but keeps its trace and now you are catalogued among other researchers. When I requested access to the Louis Graydon Sullivan papers, that act entered me into a shadowy procession of trans men, collectively wearing a path through the library carpet as we searched for our stories in someone else's diaries. Years before, when I handed over my credentials to get midcentury novelist Ann Bannon's papers, I had found myself standing in a spiritual library-line among lesbians hungry to enter and be entered by her fictions. We're all in ghost-trails misting through another. Identity coalesces and disperses simultaneously in our encounters with the dead. Our paths are indistinct and accidental; but wherever we would wander, archives have strict, arcane, and necessary rules about who can step where. The solid-time archivist was tapping his fingers for my signature and driver's license. I handed myself over. Nothing personal; it's his job to certify who I am so he can track me down if I do anything to harm our collective past.

> Once bodies had been interred and their flesh had decomposed,
> skeletal parts were often moved around, sometimes being relocated
> in complex and formal ways.[35]

After 5000 years, nobody knows who decided which bones in which barrows belonged where, who helped them disaggregate, who moved the parts around.

Many years ago, after social transition and before hormones, I volunteered at the GLBT Historical Society. It was above the comics museum on Mission just past SF Dancewear, where I used to buy my tango shoes. One day the salesclerk gave me shine for being brave enough to wear the high heels made for following men, and topped it off with extra credit because I had the baby with me. She was inviting me into some poorly-thought-through variant on sisterhood. I didn't want to get into gender politics with her so I gritted my trans feminist teeth into a smile, shoved my new dance shoes into the stroller, carried the whole assemblage upstairs to the archives. I was excavating the prehistory of the Historical Society. Buried on a low shelf I'd found a box of cassette tapes from the San Francisco Lesbian and Gay History Project's meetings. The archivist hesitated. Professional protocol said to hold them back; they'd never been accessioned and who knew what they might contain; but eventually I wangled permission to listen in exchange for digitizing the tapes.

I signed a stack of forms and settled into the sound of the '70s. Inside the headphones, my skull filled with hiss and crackle so that I felt that I was eavesdropping from the future; and then it was July of 1979. In late June the History Project had staged a public slide lecture called "Lesbian Masquerade." It presented community historian Allan Bérubé's research on 19th century "passing women," a.k.a. people assigned female at birth who chose to live and work and fuck as men. (More on that later.) Lou Sullivan was in the house. Excited and moved and willing to bet that some of those "passing women" weren't women at all, he set out to find his trancestors. But there were bad fairies at the slideshow that night, who took a different path away from the event. They raised fences around lesbian gender and desire, staked signs to warn men out, and took offense because nobody had asked their permission before treading what they now claimed as womyn's land. Vengeful in July these fairies came to the History Project with weapons in their mouths. They said those graves belonged to them. They drew battlelines in the midsummer meadow where Lou had passed only days before. The long grass was blowing on the hill where his dead beloved once stood, looking out to sea.

I took the headphones off in the archive of now. I was as tired as though I'd been listening to my parents fighting over custody. It's inevitable that I take sides. I believe that some were wronged and some were in the wrong, and I can back my historical judgment here with evidence.

Those citations are written in blood. And yet my loyalties don't change the fact that nobody in that conversation would have mobilized to take me in, recognized me as one of theirs. On my lap my infant daughter fussed to nurse. I closed my laptop, opened my shirt, and felt her settling warm between my chest and the building tension in the History Project.

We're still going over and over the same damaged ground, old KEEP OUT signs made newly lurid with fresh paint. These days the trans-exclusionary radical feminists insist that they alone may decide who women are and what they want to become. By 1973, this destructive and arrogant version of feminism was already targeting trans lesbians in the US. By the summer of 1979, when a handful of righteous lesbian-feminists followed up on "Lesbian Masquerade" by asserting their watchdog presence at the History Project's meetings, they had an army behind them to enforce their rules of access to lesbian identity, culture and desire among both the living and the dead. No boys allowed.

We all make choices about which ancestors we carry with us and which bodies we'd rather bury deep. So much is at stake. Right of access and right of transfer; youngman Zach was looking for a shortcut through the convoluted politics of trying to publish selections from Lou Sullivan's diaries, and I said mmm-hmm, mmm-hmm, pondering how people keep arguing about property lines, why they think they can halt the ancestors in their tracks.

But the dead like to dance
and lines are mobile wandering things.

My people have always hated sitting still. Some Neolithic barrows hold
over 9,000 pieces of bone yet lack the skulls you'd need to give everybody
a head. Other barrows hold nothing but skulls and longbones worn by
weather and beasts. We don't know exactly what happened but certainly
these are the kinds of injuries you risk when you go gallivanting around
the British Isles in the Neolithic without your flesh coat, for goodness
sake. What terrible archival procedure—but excellent for networking.

The ancient ones walked in turf trails their feet engraved as they followed
the lay of the land, the flow of water, the shifts of sun and fog and forage.
When paths crossed, the living might have clashed and killed, but if the
time and place and trust were right, they might just as well have made
camp side by side and swapped stories by shared fires. Maybe that's when
the bones of the ancestors changed hands. Not as commodities, but gifts:
perhaps such choreographies of time and tenderness generated kinship
among those others who partnered with, tended to the dead. Perhaps
what mattered most were the facts of carrying and being carried, and the
line that brought you to a crossroads with the ancestors in your hands.

> The purpose of history, guided by genealogy, is not to discover the roots of our identity but to commit ourselves to its dissipation.[36]
> —Michel Foucault, "Nietzche, Genealogy, History"

It was June of 1979 when Lou Sullivan set out to find the trancestors. Several hundred years later, pockets bulging with stories, Lou circled back to the Main Library where some of the History Project members had also gathered for the first meeting of what would become the GLBT Historical Society. The earth kept circling the sun until Lou set down his final bag of bones. His breath turned to paper and landed in a box that in turn landed in Susan's archiving hands. Blue-eyed cleverfingers separated, sorted, recombined, assembled into invitations. Come love, she wrote, come share these bones. She folded her wooing into acid-free airplanes and sent them flying over San Francisco, out into broad sky. I found one of them folded into a theater program. I decoded it, swallowed its secrets, made them part of me, recombined them, sent them on their way again. They passed through other hands until they reached youngman Zach. He set out for the Big Barrow. One day he called me up to talk about the politics of community history: and there I was, picking him up in front of the Main Library in the spring of 2017.

We bone-carriers didn't necessarily choose one another as kin. We chose to tend the dead, to cut or sort or polish or carry or trade. I told Zach I think desire is something we pass along and trancestors are things we make by hand. Zach nodded. Yes, he said, like how Erik Scollon held my hands around the clay so I could feel it centering, and now I do that with my students, and sometimes I can feel Erik's hands around mine, around theirs, around the clay.

Creative lineage is something I can get behind. Some people did the carrying and some were carried; but that was millennia ago. Before recognizable lines of descent, access by permission, and acid-free archival tissues. Before citations.

When I started grad school in 1991, I read a wonderful article in which a senior feminist historian questioned the practice of claiming lesbian foremothers who would not have embraced that name. It led me to a source that I wound up using in an essay of my own, so I put a draft in an envelope and mailed it to her. Looking back, I am almost as amazed by my presumption as by the jaw-dropping generosity of her response: three single-spaced, typewritten pages of encouragement, provocation, direction. We had never met in person but she recognized me as another bone-carrier and gave me the best map she could. Decades later I ran into her voice in the archives, her crisp professionalism preserved on those unaccessioned cassette tapes of History Project meetings. Part of me wishes I could send this book to her but maybe it's just as well; I suspect she'd be horrified that I'm referring to unpublished materials without attributions or permissions.

Transcestrality is not about your genealogy, it's about the lines you make by walking. The lineage I create brings me into being as a body that has moved through this time-field. Richard Long has walked now for over half a century. I am following in his footsteps. I'm carrying bones I'll gladly share and I never know in advance what other bodies I'll encounter, nor who might be resting at the meadow's edge in the shade of a tall green mound.

Zach keeps reminding me that yes, our paths are worth the time they take. Art is what time is for.

Love makes many kinds of chains. They connect, they are plural, their bodies are composite and wandering. Each one embodies the potential for another linkage elsewhere, elsewhen. In the spring of 2017, I picked Zach up in front of the San Francisco Main Library. Backwards and forwards, in galleries and dive bars, over bridge and bay and underpass. Forging connections with our feet and careful tongues. Circling around Lou Sullivan. Taking the long way home.

Skip to my Lou, my darling.

A CHARM: Marrow

Bones are partly liquid, did you know that? After you die, only the hard parts are left behind, their grooves and spirals rich with information about how you lived. This is possible because the fluid that is part of bones' living structure picks up signals from the dynamic external environment—everything from the mineral content of your drinking water to the way you carry your backpack—and translates those signals to the cells that have the machinery to remodel bone tissue from within. It's a process that won't be rushed: but if you are patient with surfaces you can tunnel into depths. Skin wants to open. You can teach an asshole to relax and a cunt to spread. We are channels made of membranes. They're a little jumpy if they don't know you, but once you make friends it's easy to drop by for a visit. Come on in, where've you been sweetheart? Please make yourself at home. Spend a minute spend a night. Maybe you recall hesitating when that cute guy across the bar smiled. You weren't sure what he was offering, or how to say yes without words. Maybe you remember bumping noses when you first practiced kissing. The youthful struggle to arrange the extra arm between two bodies in bed. Repetition builds technique. Opening gets less and less awkward until you can fall into a stranger's arms and look permeable doing it. Trying not to wonder if he'll freak out when he touches your strange junk. Trying not to worry about what's circulating in his blood. Trying not to wonder whether you'll wind up carrying his bones.

FIFTH LINK:
Danse Macabre

By the time I arrived in San Francisco Lou wasn't skipping anywhere. He died of AIDS-related illness in the spring of 1991.

Professional truth-teller Sarah Schulman opens her history of ACT UP New York by saying,

> This is an apocalyptic story of the first generation of AIDS activists, who experienced the virus in a way that no subsequent generation would ever have to experience it again . . . Some people went on to find a place in the world; some lost their place forever. [But] only these survivors carry the burden of the first years of the mass death experience that was AIDS.[37]
> —Sarah Schulman, *Let the Record Show:*
> *A Political History of ACT UP New York, 1987–1993*

She should know. She shoulders that weight and I once heard a man say that he didn't really know what it was like; he can't imagine the epicenter, because he'd only lost two lovers and his best friend. Two of those three precious people, in the same six months. My mind won't wrap around it. And yet, and yet. Apocalypse is not containable. You didn't have to go to a funeral a week to be rocked by the epidemic. To be shaken by the fear of getting sick, yes, but also by that enormous, devastating indifference to queer death. The real glee at our destruction.

I hear endless news stories of murder around the nation where the
defendant claims self-defense because this queer tried to touch
him and the defendant being freed and I'm lying here on this bed
of Peter's that was the scene of an intense illness and the channel
of the TV has been turned to some show about the cost of AIDS
and I'm watching a group of people die on camera because they
can't afford the drugs that might extend their lives and some fella
in the healthcare system in texas is being interviewed—I can't even
remember what he looks like because I reached through the television
screen and ripped his face in half—he's saying, "If I had a dollar to
spend for health care I'd rather spend it on a baby or an innocent
person with some illness or defect not of their own responsibility;
not some person with AIDS . . ." and I recall Philip's description
of finding someone he knew almost dead on a bench in Tompkins
Square Park because no hospital would take him in because he had
AIDS and no health insurance and I read the newspaper stories about
the politician in Arizona saying on the radio, "To solve the problem of
AIDS just shoot the queers . . ." and his press secretary claimed the
governor just didn't know the microphone was on and besides they
didn't really think this would affect his chances for reelection.[38]

—David Wojnarowicz, *Close to the Knives*

Straight loathing was nothing new. Long before HIV came along, we
queers served as cultural icons for moral contagion and the destruction
of all meaningful social ties. The 1970s Gay Liberation movement
empowered many of us to reframe those accusations. We turned rejection
into an open door and danced on through. The politicians hated us all
the more for refusing shame at our exclusion from the institutions called
Marriage and The Family. For a decade, many of us didn't care. We were
too busy fucking a new world into being.

Alongside the dismal toll of death, what many of us have lost is a
culture of sexual possibility: back rooms, tea rooms, movie houses,
and baths; the trucks, the piers, the ramble, the dunes. Sex was
everywhere for us, and everything we wanted to venture: golden
showers and water sports, cocksucking and rimming, fucking and fist
fucking. Now our untamed impulses are either proscribed once again
or shielded from us by latex.[39]

—Douglas Crimp, *"Mourning and Militancy"*

78

That story both is and isn't mine. I was too young and too female to make it through the gay men's tearoom doors. In 1981, when men in New York, LA, and San Francisco began dying from what was then called Gay Related Immune Deficiency, I was in Tennessee practicing tongue kissing with my 8th grade girlfriends. In 1983, when I started sneaking into gay bars, I'd developed a tiny waist and thighs I couldn't stuff into the Wranglers that filled men's rooms in the truck stops on my teenage Southern highways. Besides, the threat of rape and murder was always near for slutty girls so I didn't have a world of possibility to lose. I was too young and too female, but I know the grief of flesh wrenched away from itself. My sex was always already gendered impossible, lust's open fields foreclosed: so different from the men outside the shuttered baths, yet like them cast in the image of loss.

What kind of inheritance is the sound of empty rooms? What kind of legacy is a barrier or an absence? You don't have to go to a funeral a week to feel a culture die. Your chain can snap in one place, in a dozen, every link dangling or dented or destroyed—these are different experiences, yet each is an experience of breaking. Watching the chain disintegrate while you're standing there with your little link in your hand.

Six hundred years ago, bubonic plague and leprosy, hunger and war engraved the Reaper's grim portrait on bodies and buildings throughout Europe. Apprentices ground minerals into pigments and mixed them with vegetable oils or horse-hoof glue. Painters reached to spread earth's colors high on charnel-houses and church walls. Did these artists think about the mud in the churchyard while they worked? Engravers bent to carve wooden blocks and press ink into soft, thick pages made of linen rags. Did they think about shrouds? They drew Death's long thin hands that clutch popes and kings, knights and merchants, monks and peasants, dragging them into round dances and great reels. Historians like to tell us these images hold a subtle class critique. Death, they say, is the great leveler and maybe so, maybe so but we don't all fall the same. Five hundred years ago, Aztec artists painted great codices that show their people dying of smallpox and measles. No dances there. No sly digs at conquistadors or priests, no images of those armored ones laid low. The codices' color gets sparser as you turn the pages. Some historians say the artists were showing us the life of the people leaching out of them. The people end as the book closes. Reeling in terror, vanishing into white space on the page—different images for different vectors of vulnerability, but however it visits you, Death comes for us all, as political as archives.

Probably the most quoted line from Lou Sullivan's diaries reads: "I took a certain pleasure in informing the gender clinic that even though their program told me I could not live as a gay man, it looks like I'm going to die like one." *Fuck you, gatekeepers*, he was saying. *I slipped through your police lines; the deed's done.* His rhetoric is masterful, but its discursive context has changed. These days young transqueers in the blogosphere and in the Bay quote Lou's line with melancholy triumph. They mean to honor their debt to him: they know Lou's commitment to becoming gay created the possibility for their own creative forms of trans embodiment. I'm glad they care. Still, it makes me wince when they take his gallows humor literally. They sound like they think he meant that getting sick made him more of a gay man. I worry nobody pointed out to them that trans women died of AIDS (still do) and HIV did not turn them into gay men (still doesn't). Sometimes it sounds like they imagine that AIDS was the magic that liberated the gayness in Lou so that it flew about in clouds of golden sparkles, distributed on the wind, sprinkles on them like a benediction, anointing them as his cultural heirs.

Youngman Zach calls this the myth of St. Lou the Martyr, who died in the fight to save trans people from compulsory heterosexuality. Sure, he says, Lou was an activist, he wanted to make things easier on us. Sure he had understandable moments of wallowing, but he wasn't given to tragic self-inflation. He was a faggot slut with a dry sense of a humor and a jewelry fetish of impressive proportions. Zach had St. Lou medals made and gave them away promiscuously to anyone who would take him up on the offer. He took a certain pleasure in getting so many guys to wear the slender golden chains that made Lou's flipper twitch. He wanted to activate a lighter, sexier side of transfag lineage: the backside of the medal says "Our Father of Open Gates." But the medal was too subtle for its audience. Lots of guys received the medals not as sexy jokes but as sacred relics. I turn mine over in my palm, remember Lou was raised Catholic, think about dancing skeletons and saints and martyrs.

New York photographer Peter Hujar (1934–1987) was raised Catholic. He went to Italy, took pictures in the antique catacombs at Palermo, came home and paired those dead bodies with portraits of his living friends. His creative heir David Wojnarowicz was raised Catholic too. When Hujar died Wojnarowicz brought cameras to the deathbed. He made mortuary portraits of Hujar's head and feet and hands, his slightly open eyes and mouth, his darkening nails. The face reminds me of Hans Holbein's 1520 painting of the dead Christ laid out on a slab, emaciated and turning green, a stark confrontation with the realities of martyrdom and decay. The hands and feet show no stigmata. I'm guessing Wojnarowicz did not believe Jesus rose from the dead. I'm guessing he knew Holbein carved the most beautiful, most elaborate danse macabre of them all. I'm guessing he knew Holbein died of the plague.

After Hujar's death, Wojnarowicz moved into his loft. He watched TV in Peter's bed and used his darkroom. A major text-and-image work called *Untitled (Hujar Dead)* (1988–1989) deploys the mortuary portraits of Hujar's disarticulated head, hands, and feet. Repeated over and over, arranged neatly across and down the paper, the multiplied body parts create the impression of a mass grave. Over that horrifying yet tender field, Wojnarowicz silkscreened text: "If I had a dollar to spend for healthcare I'd rather spend it on a baby or innocent person with some defect or illness not of their own responsibility . . ." Wojnarowicz repeated those words on other images, and again in his memoir *Close to the Knives*. I repeated them above. Repetition is the point. So many bodies, so many bits. All the straight smugness, all the queer rage. Over and over again. All the pieces coming apart. Every available dollar spent to prevent babies from growing into a queer future with any kind of past. Let all the sickos die in the name of The Family. Rip that politician's face in half. Surround Hujar's dismembered corpse with a border made of cut-up money: the early Christian martyrs were thrown to the lions because they would not worship the Roman emperor as a god.

Some skulls are in fragments.

.

The brutal fact is that politicians and bureaucrats and insurance lobbyists murdered Lou Sullivan along with hundreds of thousands of faggots and whores and junkies of his generation. People were thrown away and then The Family came along to steal their bodies and lied and lied and lied about their motives and the cause of death. Not all families, of course not, and Lou's loved him well but The Family? Oh hell no.

Q: What's the hardest part of finding out you have AIDS?
A: Trying to convince your parents you're a hemophiliac.

Hahahahahahahahaaaaaaaaaa

But about St. Lou: let's keep martyrdom in political perspective. In mid-November 1993, the CDC published updated cumulative data on HIV/AIDS-related deaths for the years Lou Sullivan and David Wojnarowicz died. In 1992 HIV/AIDS killed roughly 33,500 people in the US. It was the leading cause of death among men aged 25-44, and the fourth leading cause of death for women in the same age bracket. AIDS-related death rates were three times higher for Black men than white men, 12 times higher for Black women than white women.

I try to comprehend these numbers by stacking sugar cubes to represent coffins. Three Black men died for every white man. Every white woman's corpse lies beside a dozen Black women. I'm not sure who's in which coffin, trans people weren't counted before 2009 as far as I can tell, and it's hard to compare numbers because HIV prevalence is now measured in new diagnoses rather than in deaths, but epidemiologists sum up the situation thus:

> Transgender people also experience factors related to stigma and marginalization that may increase their vulnerability to HIV infection, including discrimination and/or victimization, homelessness, incarceration, lack of healthcare insurance or healthcare access, mental health issues, suicidal ideation or attempts, and unemployment/underemployment.[40]
> —Hollie Clark et al., *Diagnosed HIV Infection in Transgender Adults and Adolescents: Results from the National HIV Surveillance System, 2009–2014*

No surprise that trans Black women are terribly over-represented relative to their numbers in the population as a whole. Nauseated, I throw the box of sugar cubes away. Then I realize what I've done, scramble to fish them out of the trash and stand there crying, paralyzed by metaphor. How white of me.

Recently I lurked on a social media thread where some young trans queers were trying to come to terms with the scale of the epidemic in the '80s. They decided that it was slimy to focus on sex in the face of such devastation. But what did they imagine Lou Sullivan wanted to live for, if not a chance to suck off pretty strangers in the park? Why invoke mythic ancestors who do nothing with their flesh but die? The young ones didn't hear their own smug superiority. They didn't realize they were replicating a straight cultural legacy of contempt for anyone who embodies the sins of the flesh.

This is not a reprimand. This is a call to arms.
This is not a lecture; it's a lifeline.

Reach back to the swollen mind and throbbing veins of political uprising. In 1988 ACT-UP staged a major action at the FDA. People went to Washington, laying their bodies on the line to change the way drug trials work in this country. In what has become an iconic image of the times David Wojnarowicz painted a sign on the back of his jacket. It said IF I DIE OF AIDS — FORGET BURIAL — JUST DROP MY BODY ON THE STEPS OF THE F.D.A.

In 1992 ACT-UP staged the first Ashes Action, where people launched their loved ones' ashes over the White House fence to scatter on the nation's front lawn. David Wojnarowicz was there in a little plastic bag. A few weeks later Mark Lowe Fisher (1953–1992) of ACT UP New York told the world to "bury me furiously."

> My friends and I have decided we don't want discreet memorial services. . . . I want my death to be as strong a statement as my life continues to be. I want my own funeral to be fierce and defiant, to make the public statement that my death from AIDS is a form of political assassination. [41]

Trans queers! Seize your life back from professionals who are as pathologizing as they are indifferent: make a body fierce and defiant: this is your trans history too.

In 1993 the direct-action transsexual advocacy group Transgender Nation disrupted the American Psychiatric Association's annual conference in San Francisco. That summer Susan wrote an essay that has become iconic as a foundation text for trans theory. In it she performs the political and analytic power of transgender rage:

> I live daily with the consequences of medicine's definition of my identity as an emotional disorder. Through the filter of this official pathologization, the sounds that come out of my mouth can be

summarily dismissed as the rantings of a diseased mind. . . . Rage
colors me as it presses in through the pores of my skin, soaking in
until it becomes the blood that courses through my beating heart. It
is a rage bred by the necessity of existing in external circumstances
that work against my survival.[42]

**Susan Stryker, "My Words to Victor Frankenstein
Above the Village of Chamounix"**

Children, pass down our furious legacy. We who have been defined as
moral illnesses and mental disorders made manifest—we need rage to
surf on, or be drowned.

The living wanted to dance with each other, not the dead. They wanted to laugh and flirt and make art and make trouble and go a-roving down by the river. Some knelt where the land ends. Their eager tongues lapped like the water below. Their knees got as dirty as their minds and then they stood, circled back around the piers to do it all again. They didn't sign up to be burdened with bones other than their own. The skulls got heavier, and they got weaker, until their skinny fingers splayed loose and open. Nobody planned to catch the weight of falling bodies.

In 1990, when he and Lou Sullivan were both at the close of their young lives, Wojnarowicz made a text-and-image piece called *When I Put My Hands On Your Body*. This time the background is a photograph he took of a desecrated Native burial mound. In 1920s Illinois, a white man excavated a Neolithic Mississipian burial complex on 'his' family farm and put 237 skeletal ancestors on display.[43] Over the image of those ancient graves, Wojnarowicz silkscreened text that begins: "When I put my hands on your body on your flesh I feel the history of that body. Not just the beginning of its forming in that distant lake but all the way beyond its ending." As in *Hujar Dead*, the text and image work together to produce a kind of tender horror; but this time the background image of Hujar's beloved corpse is replaced by a background made of dead "Indians."

The first time I saw this piece I looked away. It hurt to imagine this artist I revere standing with his camera among the other tourists, looking and clicking as though at mastodon bones, as though these skeletons were relics of an extinction in the passive voice. As though genocides were meteors and civilizations fall like leaves after frost. Native American and Indigenous studies scholars call this the fantasy of the "vanishing Indian." In this fantasy, actual Indigenous people just sort of fade away, conveniently opening both conceptual and geographic space for white Americans to insert ourselves as their successors. For four hundred years white settlers have reframed invasion as inheritance, claiming the mantle of indigeneity in all its (alleged) primitive purity, timelessness, and freedom.[44]

There's no question that the text of *When I Put My Hands on Your Body* mobilizes these tropes in its opening lines, which locate life and death simultaneously in the artist's loving hands and in a landscape immune to history. Nonetheless, Wojnarowicz's conventional romanticization of Native death co-exists with his consistent refusal to naturalize genocide. One of his last paintings, *Americans Can't Deal with Death* (1990), underscores his conviction that death is always already political. *Americans* is a huge close-up of a hanging cluster of orchid buds, the tip of each unopened flower dipped in red. Wojnarowicz stitched a pair of small photographs to the canvas with matching red thread. The first photograph shows a head in a gas mask, helmet looming like a mushroom and eye holes black and blank, oh hello there, Death, you again, hiding in war's plain sight. The other returns to the ancient mounds. The black pits of its opened graves repeat the black pits of the gas mask. Sequenced left to right, paired in their capillary frames against the hothouse flower, these photographs prompt us to see the soldier and the skeletons as bound in the asymmetrical partnership of empire and massacre.

We are being solicited to recognize state-sponsored murder as both intentional and profitable: across the top of the painting a block of text begins "Americans can't deal with death unless they own it." Yet Wojnarowicz's use of those ancestral bones replicates an element of the very violence, the very commodification, he sought to highlight and critique. There's no possibility of resolution here. His flesh is long beyond its ending. I want to run my fingers over his printed words. I am feeling for the trace of the artist's hands in the ink he left behind, wishing I could go dig my nails into the White House lawn, wondering why I think I have the right to claim him as my dead to mourn. Indigenous activists finally got those desecrated mounds closed to public view in the spring of 1992, 110 days before Wojnarowicz died.

Things circle back around and nothing is ever entirely pure.

When I touch your body I feel the history of that body. When I touch your body I take apart your bones to make more room for art and flame. When I touch your body I stretch you past the end of longing. When I touch your body I leave the marks of stories I carry in my hands. I want you to feel that you belong to a people who flowered in resistance. I want you to carry on this legacy where rage and grief stretch into carnal joy.

I tried to arrange for juicy youngman Zach to be touched by leathermen who had stored the memory of Lou's body in their own. But all Lou's lovers are dead, so the best I could do was take him to meet plague survivors, men who were there, in the bars and dungeons. We made the most of it. On the long road home from an exhausting weekend Zach finally asked me, "Where is *your* body in all this?"

this page intentionally left blank

Well-settled into middle age, stabilized by childbearing and testosterone, I no longer shift shape faster than the eye can follow. Go ahead and look at me. I'm wiry from decades of dancing, losing my hair, still good at slipping through a crowd. Dykes don't recognize me anymore but my lips recall the butches of my adolescence. What more can I say about this body, positioned as I am between the princeling I wasn't quite, and the old leathermen whose fleshly past I partly share? This chapter is trying to recreate a world my kind inherited sideways. I survived a plague that raged on the other side of the bathhouse door and down the hall. The men Lou Sullivan sucked didn't see me coming, but their stories are inextricably entwined with mine, both in kinship and in its refusal.

Bad boundaries have a bad reputation but hard-drawn lines have caused me more heartache. Personally, I never learned to like the taste of latex. Once you've loosened up your buttons, locking down again is a tremendous physical stress as well as a psychic violation. Reasonable precautions can so easily become a tragic habit of rigidity and mistrust and oh, I understand, I truly do. Yes opening is risky; but that's life, and you won't get AIDS from the ancestors anyway so go ahead, beckon the dead to your table, to your door. Let them take your cigarette, unzip your jeans without assuming you know how they're going to move you. Libraries and bedrooms, dungeons and cars; kissing and cocksucking, flogging and phone sex, figure it out as you go.

Shortly after Peter Hujar died and Wojnarowicz tested positive, he began to make the *Sex Series (for Marion Scemama)* (1989–1990), untitled bird's-eye photographs of devastated places. New York's Lower East Side, a tornado-torn prairie, a train on tracks scarring the dry buttes of the Southwest, paratroopers drifting below their bomber toward the ground: all printed in negative, like X-rays, so that their dominant images glow silvery against black backgrounds and all nuances of shadow turn into thin cobwebs of light. The tense and ghostly landscapes are inset with little circular close-ups cropped from Hujar's vintage porn archives. The *Sex Series* shows the loss of sexual joy as inseparable from the loss of all those beloved men. Wojnarowicz told Cynthia Carr, his friend and biographer, that he made these prints because he wanted "some sexy images on the wall—for me. To keep me company. To make me feel better."[45] Those inset circles are akin to peepholes, or portals into pools brimming with intimacy and pleasure. They make the occasional inset appearance of soldiers, a car wreck, or the crucified Christ within the scene feel even bleaker and more heartbreaking.

Peter Hujar was buried in Gate of Heaven Cemetery, the Roman Catholic graveyard outside of New York City. Lou Sullivan was cremated and his ashes were sprinkled into the Pacific outside San Francisco Bay. David Wojnarowicz was cremated and his ACT UP friends hurled his ashes over the cast-iron fence that keeps the public off the White House lawn.

A CHARM: Data

In 1993 the CDC recorded 103,691 cases of AIDS in the United States, including Puerto Rico. Of these, 14,795 were in people 25–29 years old.

In 1993 I turned 26.

In 1993 the CDC revised its definition of AIDS cases to include opportunistic infections, including those more common among women. Case numbers went up 127%.

In 1993—even after the revision—the CDC noted that HIV-related deaths were significantly underreported, estimating that between 25% and 33% of the people who died of AIDS were not included in the overall count.

In 1993 I had four different temporary addresses and either three or four girlfriends, depending on your metric. I did not have the necessary swimming skills.

In 1993 the San Francisco Department of Public Health reported 1788 deaths from AIDS.

In 1993 I helped throw fifteen LINKS parties serving roughly fifty people at each one. (We never tallied the condoms and gloves; Edward and I got boxes of them for free from Public Health Center #1 in the Castro.)

In 1993 my eleven-year-old old truck, Betsy, and I could cover the 429 miles from Irvine to San Francisco in just under eight hours, including a stop to let her engine cool down.

In 1993 my adjusted gross income was $12,883.11, of which $601.88 came from making sex toys for gay leathermen and the rest from teaching modern US history at the University of California, Irvine.

In 1993 I witnessed a co-worker at the leather factory deteriorate, and eventually die, at his workbench two feet away from mine. I doubt he was 40.

In 1993 Transgender Nation disrupted the American Psychological Association annual conference in San Francisco.

In 1993 my gender dysphoria was so bad I sometimes lost entire days just trying to get dressed.

In 1993 two of my friends killed themselves rather than keep living as the women they knew they weren't.

In 1993 I skipped meals to cover the femme girls' door fee at Club Junk, which was $3 if you got there before 7 pm. My dates thought it was romantic that I was always there early.

In 1993 I did not die. Instead, I danced three times a week.

A CHARM: Enchaînement, connection

I cannot count the times my heart and skin have softened, nor all the lips I've kissed; but I can chant my most important lovers' names.

Words don't have roots. They don't connect in stillness underground. Mobile, they sing and sway, like kelp or rigging in the wind. The names we give each other twine past and present with here and there, into ropes and chains of meaning that knot and coil and cable; fold and ply, link and fray and splice and split until they arrive at last, in you, with all their storied lineage aboard. From tongue to ear. You pass them on.

> In French, whenever a word ending in a consonant sound is followed by a vowel . . . that consonant sound is transferred onto the next word. This euphonic technique is called enchaînement and it's one of the aspects of French pronunciation that sometimes makes it difficult to determine where one word ends and the next begins.[46]
> —Laura Lawless, *Lawless French, s.v. "Enchainement/Liaison"*

Words like memories flow beyond all bounds, transferring their affections in endless minglings of sound and sense. Listen:

Plié, folded
Tendu, reaching
Tombé, fallen

In ballet-speak *enchaînement* means a series of steps linked together to form a phrase. Euphony and metaphor, music and movement. We count as we dance. A properly constructed phrase flows through the body so that each gesture sets up the next. Landing on the beat—

Plié is kin with *ply* like rope, three strands twisted to a purpose, pliable as it twines around two willing wrists. *Plié* is a word for folding toward the floor. We melt through planes of motion, live geometry in time: *plié* is a word for when the line between your thighs becomes a sweet and open diamond.

Tombé transitions. It is a yielding to gravity and trust in which the dancer falls from one leg to the other, or from two legs onto one. It's a beautiful statement of traveling away from your upright self in order to experience a soft landing.

Tendu comes from the French verb *tendre*, to reach or stretch. In English to have a *tendre* used to mean you yearned for someone, hoped to hold them tenderly. Two become one. From the outside *tendu* seems predictable, even dry: a leg extends in a straight line from hip to toe and here to there: point A to point B. From the inside, however, *tendu* is a relationship and the essence of expansion. It's joyful integration. It's the leaving without which there is no possibility of return.

Technically *tendu* is a visible outcome of double femoral rotation, one thigh spiraling clockwise, one against the clock, organized in calibrated tensions that assign stability to one leg and mobility to the other. Drill down into the floor, the subfloor, the foundations. The muscles engage under my ass, wrapping through the channel where leg meets labia at the bottom of my body to bring my inner thigh forward. Keep spiraling. I'm doubled and helical from tear duct to talus joint. Don't clench the channel; anchor, anchor that heel into rocky bottom. Keep spiraling. I'm so powerfully connected now that one leg can hold my crown into the night and the other blossoms in response. The free leg's foot slides along the floor longer, longer, as wide as the perineum can spread, twisting like starlight until the heel simply must lift or the rest of me must follow, displacing my axis; but if you stay solid on your standing leg and extend long through your arch, if you keep going and going, eventually your toes will *dégager*, disengage, lift off the ground on which we stand. When you are at full stretch and before you take the air, neither leaving nor returning, at that point you are *en tendu*. Reaching. No promises.

But aren't there always memories? And expectations?

Form persists as meaning changes. We inherit rules for how to hold for one or two or three, when to flex and stretch and let ourselves go. We enact them in our daily choreographies, the minute rituals and grand chains whose traces can survive in us for centuries. Whose ancient paths we tread.

Plié, a fold. *Tendu*, a stretch or reach.
I soften toward you; I give you my attention;
I am building tension toward a fall.

98

SIXTH LINK:
Sister, down

Once upon a time I moved from a genre I was assigned to one I made for myself. Historians learn to be cautious about identifying with the past lives we study, like ethnographers learn to cross-check the oral histories they gather. I could have sworn I came out into Macon's bar scene around 1983, but some very reputable scholars have dated my memory to the late 1950s, a decade before I was born.[47] I'd like to be able to defer to their well-researched professional consensus. Truth is, though, my bones are brimming with tales of the teenage sexual underground in the early 1980s, when AIDS came slamming into central Georgia like a runaway semi. Believe me or don't, your call. When I left the South, I didn't bring documentary evidence with me. All I can say is we're all unreliable witnesses.

This is not testimony. This is a murder ballad.

There was the time my redheaded 10th grade US Lit teacher had a student stand on a chair and hold a notebook against the two-way inter-com, just in case, while she whispered the urgent news that Walt Whitman was a homosexual. She could have lost her job. When I was in ninth grade Michael Hardwick was arrested for sodomy in his own Atlanta bedroom, and in 1986, the United States Supreme Court upheld Geor-gia's right to criminalize oral and anal sex between consenting adults, affirming that perverts have no right to privacy.[48] Charis Books & More, a regional feminist hub since 1975, was only a couple of hours up I-75. It sold lesbian novels and labrys pendants and pins with double woman symbols on them, but I didn't know about it until after I'd left the state to go to college. In Macon I literally never met a visibly gay person who wasn't scraping to make ends meet in some dead-end low-status job (the closet cases made more money, but their bar tabs ran proportionately higher). Later, north of the Mason-Dixon Line, I read about dyke life before Gay Liberation, before lesbian feminism, and it seemed to me like I came out in a city without calendars. No wonder my timestamps are impossibly confused. I know I was there, but how can I claim a story that doesn't seem to have a then? Chronology doesn't do the job they said it would do.

Do you remember where this all began? In the hallucinatory gap between Trump's election and inauguration E.G. sent me the email that said: Dive in. She meant back into 1991 but I heard lesbian poet Judy Grahn calling from January 1972 instead. *You smell like the ocean I said and laid down my tongue along the dark tooth edge of sleeping.*[49] Decades later I performed that poem, in words, in public. My CV attests that in May of 2012 I was on a queer art panel at the New Museum, New York's self-described "leading destination for new art and new ideas." Afterward we all went out to party in a famous performance space. As the only trans person present, I felt I had a position to uphold in this venue where dykes were boss. My memory swelled with lesbian poetry until my mouth overflowed. In the place where her breasts come together, I began. I perched on the tall spotlit stool, hands gripping its front edge with my thighs apart, shoulders spread, doing my best to summon the confident butch lasciviousness I longed for in the '80s.

Levelling my gaze into the approving darkness, I purred *Swim, she told me. And I did, I did.*

Back in Georgia circa 1984, I was both aroused and frightened by the prospect of going to the bar called the We Three. The name seemed tastelessly blunt about perversion, six bare legs in a bed. In contrast, the Pegasus Lounge suggested transformation's easy wings. Past the dragon watchful at the door, down into the Stygian dark under a nineteenth-century brick warehouse, you opened a heavy curtain into the cave where the butterflies bloomed on a dull black stage the size of a postage stamp. Weekend men lined the walls on Tuesdays. Was I ever there on a slow night? Warm leather, poppers, and Camel Lights weaving and wafting above the steady bar smell of fermentation.

There were queens who came through Macon on a regular circuit, Miami or Fort Lauderdale to New York and New Haven. Feathered, muscular, dark, and flaunting; there was a lot of Lurex involved. They called themselves Cherry and Blackberri and we clapped and whistled and stuffed bills into firm round places and the next morning they'd have moved on. Except for Tangerine Summers, who was and remains a regional institution. After I left the South she grew a wee problem with drugs that led to other, larger problems, till the good Lord took her in his hand and led her to a better life. Tangerine's in her 60s now, still around those parts, fundraising for AIDS charities and praying a public gospel of sequins and sobriety, but the other queens who worked the Pegasus appeared and disappeared like magic. One night I was bent dizzyingly backward over a rickety wooden chair while a black-haired femme feasted on my face. Under her tongue I registered a faraway voice announcing, "Yes, folks, there it is, the Longest Kiss in History!" I felt the followspot glare even before I opened my eyes. At the other side of its circle, Cherry's grin blinded me like her sequins, only marginally less dazzling than the light itself. Her eyes met mine and again later, after her set, when she caught me cruising her in the bathroom line. She hit me with an ah-ha look. Read me as something she knew, and knew I didn't know, and got back on her game.

I wanted to get into the drag queens' dressing room so badly, imagining a world of erotic glamour in there—but there was no place for me in the narrow dark hallway that led behind the stage. And I, for sure, didn't fit in the back bar. That was where the Real Dykes hung out. The pool table under its Budweiser shade glowed a green frame for the daggers' broad strong backs as they stretched into the light. 40 years later, I can still summon the shock of longing that swept over me the first time I dared to come down the ramp from the main bar into their territory. One must have felt the lightning. She turned and looked straight at me. Read me as no threat and got back to her game.

I was underage but old enough to know I could cause trouble both for them and for me.
I knew that getting closer would undo me in some way I could not yet imagine.
I knew that was how I wanted to be undone.

"There is a concern that these people could be involved in homosexual activities or criminal activities," Police Chief Jim Brooks told *The Macon Telegraph* in a 1985 article about the arrest of a drag queen. "It is in the best interest of the community to control people from masking their identity, period." Read more here: *https://www.macon.com/news/local/ article231643068.html#storylink=cpy*

I'm gonna guess Jim Brooks was not someone with much tolerance for poetry that makes worlds, or prose that both solicits and rewards the work of interpretation. Such a pity, to turn away from a body filled with fairy tales.

Once upon a time I didn't know that people like me were commonly accused of being liars, or crazy, and that still seems ridiculous because who expects fairies to conform to everyday standards of evidence?

Steal my catskin and I am locked into a human-girl form I did not choose. Throw a blanket knitted of nettles over my back and my sister will be saved as my swan's body resolves into my ontological princeliness. Peter Pan had breasts called Mary Martin under that green leotard and she, he, they crowed with the triumph of being wonderful. Here it's cold and I'm alone so let the wind carry me at her back in a cradle woven from her long black hair to a place where I can discover the secret of my own desire. Fairies will lead you astray into their underground realms and you won't emerge unchanged: there's more than one way to tell the truth. More than one code to crack. More than one story to pass on.

Here's another tale that is and isn't mine.

She had a seventh-grade education. Quick, dark, compact, and clever, so clever; she could keep a running tally of her liquor sales for an entire shift, tracking every bar tab in her head as she went. She used to whistle through her teeth with satisfaction when she added up the slips at the end of the night and the math came out right. She was fighting with her "roommate," and it hurt enough that she got drunk and slipped, said *girlfriend*, but there's still room for ambiguity there and she still didn't name herself *gay*. She resisted my charms until they officially broke up. Then she kissed me in the walk-in but she couldn't take me to the Pegasus because her girl was there. She also couldn't take me back to their trailer until her girl moved out. Truth is, it was her trailer to begin with, but she insisted on butch courtliness and surfed couches until I finally lured her into my bed one afternoon when my mother was at work. She caught my wrists over my head. The shock lifted me, arcing, off the mattress. She held me down. She followed through.

Just before I graduated from high school, the warehouse on the corner of Cotton and Cherry burned down.

As far as I can tell, *The Macon Telegraph* documented that fire only because it also threatened to damage Nu-Way Weiners, the second hot dog stand instituted in the United States, which weirdly did end up burning to the ground, years later, in 2015. In mourning that culturally significant loss, the city paper noted that back in 1984

> A major fire destroyed the Pegasus Lounge in the basement of a four-story building at the corner of Cotton and Cherry. It is now a parking lot for SunTrust Bank. Fire Chief Marvin Riggins remembers that blaze. He battled it as a young firefighter in his early years with the department. "We were able to contain it and keep it off the Nu-Way building," he said. Read more here: *https://www.macon.com/news/local/news-columns-blogs/ed-grisamore/article30220494.html#storylink=cpy*

Flaming hot weiners, Batman! This time the faggots didn't burn, oh well. Still, all that's left of the bar I came out in is a chain-link fence blocking off cracked concrete and crumbling rebar.

After the fire, the Pegasus survived another 9 years by moving to 3rd Street toward the river—only a few blocks down, but a definite step onto skid row.

We used to act like we had hatched fully grown from golden eggs, linked and unlinked in serial forms that promised us permanence even though we knew better. Truth is, we didn't always want it to last.

After my butch's ex-girlfriend finally moved out of the trailer I tried to wheedle her into taking me home, I wanted her to fuck me in her bed but she said no, her room was so small she couldn't even change her mind in there so how could she spread my legs? She said sexysweet things that we enjoyed all the more because I was going to go north to college soon—six weeks, a month, two weeks away; then close enough for her to trust me with the knowledge of the family she'd left behind when she crossed the county line, alone, at 13. She looked at the ceiling and said she'd shot her stepfather when he started in on her little sister and the tightness in her face dared me to ask questions that we both knew I already had the answers to. Nobody ever came looking, she added. The whole town knew he had it coming. A few years ago, I found her mugshot on a Fulton County website. Drunk and disorderly, morals, or disturbing the peace? It's gone now and I can't remember. I only remember the wrenching sadness of her jawline, clenched against the camera.

Some charms aren't charming. Some charms get lost. Sometimes the dragon lays the whole island waste; the palace burns; the queens flee. Soon there's nobody left who remembers the villagers who died by fire.

In January 1993, Elizabeth Davidson drove down from Tennessee to visit friends in Macon. The 25-year-old went to the Pegasus Lounge on Third Street, one of two gay bars open at the time, and was fatally shot by 16-year-old Dion Felton, according to archives. Felton and three other teens had followed a man into the Pegasus earlier that night and were asked to leave because they were harassing patrons. The four returned 90 minutes later and Felton started shooting. Davidson was killed and another woman was shot but survived. The bar closed for good the next day. Read more here: *https://www.macon.com/news/local/ article231643068.html#storylink=cpy*

Dion Felton was convicted of malice murder, two counts of aggravated assault, and one count of simple assault. He was sentenced to life plus 20 years. That could have been the end of his story, except for his appeal up through the State Supreme Court, which heard his case in 2008.[50]

Reading the court's summary, I am struck by Felton's attempt to shove the crime onto one of his —friends? One of the guys he'd been drinking with at the bar next door; musta been a dive. Bad situation all around. Felton was only 16 at the time. I imagine he might have been a mean young snake, son of a mean old snake, raised among people with guns and an overfondness for the bottle. At age 31, he argued for release on technical grounds that ultimately attribute his arrest and conviction to law officers' illegal incompetence. I can't imagine that defense would get you very far and it did not. The appeals recorder made no mention of his conduct during those years of imprisonment, or of his youth at the time of the crime, the social significance of incomplete prefrontal cortex development at that age. Seems like nobody was on his side. Maybe that's because he stayed mean even minus the whiskey. Possibly the prison-industrial complex had no particular interest in letting his forced labor go free. Whatever; the law gets to tell his story now, and it chooses not to go into detail. All I can say with certainty is that the State of Georgia affirmed that yes, on January 14, 1993, Felton did maliciously murder Elizabeth Davidson, wound Diana Lynn Salyers, and assault, by pistol, Frances J. Ryan.

Felons are like fairies is the ease with which they vanish. I can't find anything in the public record about these dykes. (Lesbians?) Their lives are not recoverable. But I know the myths that tell me where they belonged. I imagine these people (women?) bowing over the green baize, backs lit, taking careful aim. Felton's wildness at the Pegasus began with coins he threw on the pool table, disrupting the game. Those coins land in my mind like tiny precursors to the bullets. Their small percussions fill the cusp between before and after. They mark the moment when Felton's name began to be linked with Davidson, Salyers, Ryan.

So many of us had so many reasons not to speak about the families that raised and dropped us into circles of light over green felt tables, next to dyke hands poised firm, deliberate, calculating the angle, sinking the ball.

I wonder if Frances was called Frank and if she (he? they?) felt guilty about getting through that night without a physical scratch. I wonder if she (?) ever played pool again. I wonder if she bought a gun.

I wonder if 25 year old Elizabeth Davidson's friends knew her by that name. I wonder whether she graduated high school. I wonder whether her parents were doubly ashamed of her for getting herself murdered in that pervert bar. I wonder whether they came for her body, and how she ranked among the dead—a plaque, a headstone, a box on Mom's dresser. I hope she didn't have to drive too far. Maybe she lived close to the state line, just up 75 near Chattanooga somewhere, around where my folks retired. Maybe she'd moved up there recently. She was almost my age; it just occurred to me that we could have been at the Pegasus together some night, both jailbait with fake IDs, desperately seeking what we might become.

What bar-dyke lineage does all this place me in? These aren't stories I would have chosen for my own, but things keep circling back around and nothing is ever entirely pure. It's possible we longed for the same butches, the same queens.

I left Macon alive. She didn't: sister down.

Tendre
Tendu
Tombé

Tender, we lean and incline and stretch toward one another.

Her skin glowed brown, she smelled like green apples sharp and sweet, and she whistled through her teeth with the joy of numbers.

We fall.

A CHARM: *Tombé, temps lié*

We fall. We come undone.

> But what about *temps levé* or *temps lié*? Often *temps* when used in this way is defined as time. *Temps levé*: time lifted. *Temps lié*: time linked. These definitions do give an idea of the lifting and linking of steps [and by extension] a movement that makes up part of a whole.[51]

> Maybe all transitions are about getting somewhere other than here, now. Some strategies are more focused on the launch, others on the arrival. Once you're committed to falling you can't reverse direction or the flow of energy without embarking on a different step; but you can link time in any direction, ongoing, forever.

Temps lié is a form of the great chain of being—reimagined as steps that we trace, softly on the floor.

A CHARM: Homo again

In 2017 Oakland-based artist and all-around badass Xandra Ibarra staged— staggered?—a community performance event she called *The Hookup/Displacement/Bar Hopping/Drama Tour.*

> In an effort to resurface the "messy" and "sucio" spirits of queer Latino and lesbian ghosts from gentrified sites in San Francisco, Ibarra led strangers and friends on a bar crawl tour to five former queer Latino and Lesbian bars in San Francisco. Together the group made altars, wrote messages, imprinted their bodies, pleasures and kisses onto the phantom walls of beloved queer venues—Esta Noche (1979–2014), La India Bonita (late 70s–1996), Amelia's (1978–1991), The Lexington (1997–2015), and Osento (1979–2008). Strangers and friends occupied each location, sipped on spirits, danced in alleys, made out, and posted counterfeit "Public Notices of Application for Ownership Change" while 1990s footage of queer Latinos and Lesbians in the former bars was projected onto walls.[52]

Xandra was asking groups of survivors to revisit the collective energies of the queer moment and extend them to build a sense of connection both in the present and across time. I couldn't go; I was on parent duty that night; but the following weekend I retraced Xandra's route up Valencia St, tuning in to the throb of memory and desire embedded in the City's structures and surfaces, its sites of affirmation and transformation. My listening feet took me to the purple Victorian at 455 14th Street that had once been the navel of my world. I laid my cheek against the gritty paint of the basement fire exit.

Press as much of the front surface of
your body (palms in or out, left or right cheek)
against the wall as possible.
Press very hard and concentrate.
Form an image of yourself (suppose you
had just stepped forward) on the
opposite side of the wall pressing
back against the wall very hard. [...]
This may become a very erotic exercise.[53]

Bruce Nauman, *Body Pressure*

I was seeking connection with whatever trace of our parties might still linger in the matter of the old dungeon, vibrating in and behind that faded purple door. The building received my weight on its broad chest. I leaned in.

SEVENTH LINK:
There, then (History Project)

To chart these romances would be to name constellations
among stars that will not stay still.[54]
—T Fleischmann, *Time is the Thing a Body Moves Through*

Summer solstice, 1979. I was 11 years old and the champion frog-catcher in my tiny New England village.

That same night in San Francisco, Allan Bérubé was 30 years old, presenting an event titled "Lesbian Masquerade" at the Women's Building on 18th St between Valencia and Guerrero. When the standing ovations finally died down, Lou Sullivan, aged 25, went up to Allan and told him about his own research on women who—as many of us thought about it then—dressed, worked, and lived as men. Backstage, the dead hiked up their trousers. They were ready to move into a different story.

You could say trans history started then and there. The dead would laugh at our presumption, but in June of 1979 we were still shapeshifting like fog between the trees outside the Women's Building. After Allan's event was over some of us went around the corner for drinks at lesbian liquor entrepreneur Rikki Streicher's then-new dyke bar Amelia's (1978-1991). I was too young for "Lesbian Masquerade" but a decade later I had my first taste of full-body bondage at Amelia's, blushing sweet fundraiser confusion into my beer. The Women's Building was five minutes' walk from Modern Times Bookstore (1971-2016) in its first iteration on Sanchez, and five minutes in the other direction from the store's Valencia Street incarnation, where I bought my first copy of Foucault's *History of Sexuality Vol. 1*. In an earlier body Sleeperfreak had helped paint *Maestrapeace*, the glorious five-story mural that wraps around the Women's Building's facade. His dead name survives in its list of contributors, like how Amelia's dyke bar persists in lists of the lost queer institutions on the Valencia Street corridor in its late 20th century heyday. Like how the Latinx dance club, Esta Noche and the women's bathhouse, Osento, survive through Xandra Ibarra's performance re-creation of nights spent staggering and laughing down enchanted sidewalks with the other pervert queers.

We leave traces in the timefield as we pass, our street choreographies winding around and through one another in patterns as power-laden as any ballet, as beautiful as any boy.

Throughout the diaries, [Lou] Sullivan most frequently organized the periods of his life by his domestic spaces, usually referring to his homes by their street names. We borrowed this approach as a structuring principle for our chapters.[55]

—Ellis Martin and Zach Ozma, "Editor's Note," in *We Both Laughed in Pleasure: The Selected Diaries of Lou Sullivan, 1961–1991*

It's such a San Francisco thing to track relationships and events by location.

Amber Hollibaugh: You [Allan] were living at Guerrero and 16th.

Allan Bérubé: So the three of us [Allan, Jeffrey Escoffier, and Eric Garber] started meeting, and I knew Amber from Modern Times bookstore at 16th and Sanchez, where the laundromat is now... I had been inspired by Jonathan [Ned] Katz's book [1976] *Gay American History* to do my own research [. . .] so I went to the California Historical Society and was looking through their old scrapbooks of clippings. I found a lot of clippings of women who passed as men. And I would talk about them with Amber when I would go into the bookstore.

Amber Hollibaugh: Allan would come in and I would be at the counter and . . . he'd come up and he'd start telling me about all the clippings he found, or the little stories that he had discovered . . . And meanwhile I was always finding odd little stories, and . . . I felt like we were all very odd, that we were interested in these kind of strange stories that really our friends were not interested in at all about passing women and women who dressed like men who caught frogs.[56]

—The San Francisco Gay and Lesbian History Project [Allan Bérubé, Jeffrey Escoffier, Amber Hollibaugh, Willie Walker], interview by Terrence Kissick and Molly McGarry, October 10, 1995, New York.

I was in elementary school and a continent away but I already knew what it felt like to kneel in amphibious places. I would have wanted to know people who knew about the women who caught frogs, like I did. I'd already wrapped my proto-trans hands around patience, and stealth, and triumph; maybe I could have peeked through my fingers at what passing might mean. I would have cared.

In 1983, Women Make Movies released a 33-minute VHS version of *Lesbian Masquerade*, retitled as: *She Even Chewed Tobacco: She Drank, She Swore, She Even Courted Girls: Passing Women in 19th Century America*. It's not very well made by current standards, just a series of stills with voice-over, but in its moment its content was all that mattered.

> The Gold Rush. A new frontier. Nineteenth-century California offered women the opportunity to pioneer new roles for themselves. Meet Babe Bean, the "trouser puzzle" who escaped the hot glare of tabloid headlines by disguising herself as Jack Garland and serving in the Spanish American War. Or Jeanne Bonnet who scored a record of 22+ arrests for wearing male attire, went to prison for her indiscretions and later organized a group of prostitutes into a shoplifting ring![57]

Next in the signifying chain came the 1989 *Hidden from History*, the first anthology of lesbian and gay historical research essays, which included a text version of *She Even Chewed Tobacco*. No tabloid exuberance here; *Hidden from History* frames "passing women" as proto-feminist rebels refusing to bend before the economic and social constraints of patriarchy:

> "Passing women" succeeded in hiding their female identities from most of the world and claimed economic and political privilege enjoyed by men. . . . To call these women "lesbians" is historically inaccurate, but many actively pursued—and won—the women they loved. [58]

A LIST OF "PASSING WOMEN" MENTIONED IN *HIDDEN FROM HISTORY:*

DR. JAMES BARRY, Inspector General of Army hospitals
BILL, boilermaker, MO
JOSEPH LOBDELL, laborer, upstate NY
MURRAY HALL, politician, NYC
CHARLEY PARKHURST, Wells Fargo stagecoach driver, CA
RALPH KERWINEO, unknown, Milwaukee, WI
JEAN BONNET, charismatic frog-catcher and all-around bad
    news, San Francisco, CA
MILTON MATSON, businessman, San Jose, CA; librarian,
    San Francisco Public Library
BABE BEAN, news reporter, Stockton, CA
JACK BEE GARLAND, lieutenant, Spanish-American war;
    male nurse, San Francisco, CA
PETER STRATFORD, unknown, unknown

Names without faces, places without footprints. A swirl and a jumble of
these bare identifiers and who am I to say who loved whom, or what it
meant or means to win: all I know is that to call these people women is
historically inaccurate.

What we might say instead: they were just passing through.

Names and addresses swirl in numberless profusion. There were notes written on napkins blowing down 18th St. I stooped to pick one up. It said that history really is just one damn thing after another, but what after means is up for grabs. Later, at the bar, I pulled the past from my pocket and folded it into an origami frog.

Bill the boilermaker in Missouri was a "passing woman." We know about him because in 1900 British sexologist Havelock Ellis included Bill in his influential *Studies in the Psychology of Sex Vol 2*.

Bill struts into the chapter on "sexual inversion in women."

> She drank, she swore, she courted girls, she worked as hard as her fellows, she fished and camped; she told stories with the best of them, and she did not flinch when the talk grew strong. She even chewed tobacco. Girls began to fall in love with the handsome boy at an early period . . . With one girl who worshipped her there was a question of marriage.[59]

There are thousands of such case studies. Sexologists named us *inverts* because we turn gender upside down, *perverts* because we turn toward our desires. Most claimed that normal people develop along exactly one narrative pathway: boys learn to chew tobacco and tell smutty stories; girls worship boys; they get married and march two by two into the ark. No plot twist goes unstraightened. Some sexologists suppressed readers' desire with deliberate boredom: they drone and drone against primitive sexual freedom and its modern analog, free verse. Others were frankly unhinged. They gabbled and frothed about decadence, in literature as in life. Their eyes bulged with visions of boys languid on couches when they should be learning how to fight like men. Jeweled tortoises for no apparent reason; hermaphrodites who stride in and out of chapters for the hell of it. Syntactical variation. The recurring image of a green carnation. Episodes of passion with no before or after—*Degenerates!* they screamed. Overwhelmed by the lush lingering of our descriptions, they said we have no plot. They said we embodied the disintegration of meaning and the downfall of civilization. We're only phone numbers on napkins. Dropped links and broken watches. Meaningless fragments. Scattered limbs. Rot and despair where once the late birds sang.

Some sexologists really, really hated lists, queers, and time machines. Others, of course, indulged in all of those things.

FOUNDING MEMBERS OF THE SAN FRANCISCO HISTORY PROJECT:

ALLAN BÉRUBÉ, working-class gay community historian,
  white anti-racist labor activist, weaver
JEFFREY ESCOFFIER, independent scholar, theorist,
  publisher, sugar daddy (but that came later)
ESTELLE FREEDMAN, academic historian of women, gender,
  and sexuality
AMBER HOLLIBAUGH, working-class fierce femme leftist and
  queer organizer, memoirist, force of nature
GAYLE RUBIN, academic anthropologist of leather
  communities, theorist, wearer of ties
[WILLIE WALKER and GREG PENNINGTON . . . ERIC
  GARBER . . . What to say about them? I never met them and
  all I know about Walker is that he did way too many drugs
  and become something of a strain toward the end of his
  life.]

Some I knew well enough to hug hello. Others were people I knew
through things they'd written, or by reputation, or someone I knew knew
them, so I knew them the way I know my ex-lovers' ex-lovers. A uniquely
queer form of relatedness, to be connected because you have both loved
the same bodies, living and/or dead.

I flex my writing fingers and remember conversations that took place
when I was in 4th grade and a continent away. Allan and Amber and
the others, building community out of crumbling newspaper clippings
about women who dressed as men. I fantasize about bringing some little
scrap of folded paper to the bookstore where they met; I'd pull it out of
my pocket to lie on the counter next to the ones the other story-catchers
found. I'd tell them how I love the world they wove. I'd want them to
recognize me as one of theirs.

In 1876 the frog-catching, "cross-dressing" Jean, or Jeanne, or sometimes Jennie Bonnet was shot and killed in a roadhouse bed with a woman named Blanche, whose former pimp thus made plain his objections to Bonnet's interventions in the local sex trade.

Before there were bridges over San Francisco Bay, before Chinese laborers laid the rails that linked the country West to East and East to West, rich men gambled on getting richer by way of a local train track to be built from San Francisco down to San Jose. Daytimes, Italian and Irish muscle loaded freight onto groaning wooden boxcars headed to the City's eager markets three hours away. After dark, the line grew lively with people riding back and forth to serve or party, wheel and deal. Is that who McNamara's roadhouse was built to serve? Men too drunk or too free or just too tired to get on home, bold women and fairies who worked their beds and bars? Certainly, it was the kind of place where an immigrant sex worker and her questionable Frenchman could take a bed for the night; certainly it was the kind of place where the proprietor didn't repair the blinds. Easy enough to peep, take aim, disappear.

What if I'd been there that night? What if I'd been the one sneaking a look at Bonnet's undressing? Maybe my frog-catcher's subtle body would have blocked the glowing slit in that broken blind. Maybe that murderous pimp would have stumbled in the dark and swore. Shoved the pistol back in his belt and gone elsewhere for another drink. Maybe I'd have been the one melting back into the night, another trans pervert with a compound complex name.

Degenerate we linger
repeating for the music of it
taste, oh taste
green figs
and futures without arrival

Those dead sexologists were iffy about poetry. One said its pulse sounded too much like the heart beating. They said it was atavistic. I wonder what they thought of the Bible. As ancient in form as it is in content, it reads like a diagnostic checklist for decadent writing: episodic and repetitive fragments in many voices, on many topics, loosely assembled into patterns, apparently indifferent to any one sustained or structuring logical or narrative principle.

The Bible is also marbled with lists.

My favorite biblical lists are the begats (admittedly an acquired taste). Begats are lists of descent and filiation. They're scattered through the 24 books of the Hebrew Bible, starting at the very beginning, with the Book of Genesis, which tells stories of the creation of the world and its people. Genesis, chapter 5 opens with the line "This is the book of the generations of Adam." God creates Adam, the first man, and then Adam begat Seth, Seth begat Enos, Enos begat Cainan, and so on for 9 generations, with ritual insertion between generations that make highly improbable claims how old each man was when he sired his son, and how old he was when he died.

I know the begats sound mind-numbingly boring, but remember, remember: these were always meant to be read aloud. Give them voice and they begin to pulse the blood and bone of memory, the archives of exiles, the roster of a people's dead.

GREAT GAYS (+) IN WESTERN HISTORY (a standard 1980s list)

DAVID AND JONATHAN
SAPPHO
ALEXANDER THE GREAT
JEAN D'ARC
TCHAIKOVSKY
WALT WHITMAN
OSCAR WILDE
ELEANOR ROOSEVELT
JAMES BALDWIN

TRANSGENDER WARRIORS (collated off the web)

JEAN D'ARC
CHEVALIER D'ÉON
JENNIE JUNE
LILI ELBE
CHRISTINE JORGENSEN
MICHAEL DILLON
SYLVIA RIVERA
MARSHA P. JOHNSON
LOU SULLIVAN
SUSAN STRYKER

The Bible's First Book of Chronicles is nothing but begats, beginning with the first man, whose name was Adam. Seven chapters in, the chanter pauses for one human moment to name two boys killed young: "And Ephraim their father mourned many days, and his brethren came to comfort him."

We all need kin to call on when we weep. Nine generations is not too much.

In 1928 Radclyffe Hall's novel *The Well of Loneliness* held up a melancholic's mirror to reflect the gloomiest possible vision of the author's lesbian circle. The novel follows Stephen, a slim-hipped person awkwardly, improbably, assigned female at birth. Early on, we get to peep into Stephen's father's study. He's been staying up half the night reading sexology—a cue that something queer is in the wind; and so it is, wafting from salon to street and back again, for another 51 short, bleak chapters. At the end Stephen has a vision of queers thronging, swirling in the wind like origami frogs, demanding that she [sic] give them voice.

> Who were they, these strangers with the miserable eyes? And yet, were
> they all strangers? Surely that was Wanda? And someone with a neat
> little hole in her side— Jamie clasping Barbara by the hand; Barbara
> with the white flowers of death on her bosom. Oh, but they were
> many, these unbidden guests, and they called very softly at first and
> then louder. . . . The walls fell down and crumbled before them; at
> the cry of their suffering the walls fell and crumbled: "We are coming,
> Stephen—we are still coming on, and our name is legion . . ."[60]

Radclyffe Hall had a decadent imagination, atrocious politics, an androgynous name, and a secure grasp of Biblical forms. Hall wore trousers and elegant gentlemen's linens. Their friends and lovers called them John. They demanded the right to their existence.

Names listed on a fridge, doodled on napkins
looking for the noun that says
becoming

Whose story is this again? I was already my town's champion frog-catcher in 1977, when the first generation of gay community historians was gathering snippets of information on the people Allan called "passing women" and Lou thought of as "female transvestites." In 1985 I learned that I had something called "male identification." Or maybe that was about the butch dykes who dazzled me? I couldn't quite figure out how that worked, but Reg the bartender who rocked my Georgia bed had absolutely zero interest in the bicoastal lesbian-feminist analysis that had inspired my new political qualms. Those only lasted ten minutes anyway. I shut up and lay back, surrounded by the scent of her strong dark curls, sharp and sweet like green apples, earthy like the tree.

> Amber Hollibaugh: And the Women's Building had a huge room that held . . . 250–300 people and we thought God, why did we take such a big room. Like who's going to come to "Lesbian Masquerade"? By a guy, put together by the Lesbian and Gay History Project, a co-gendered project in the middle of separatism in San Francisco at the Women's Building. [. . .] [All] of us were stunned because we got there and there were lines around the block.[61]

Midsummer's eve of 1979 is the only recorded occasion on which Lou Sullivan's search for trancestors led him to enter a lesbian lineage: he stood in the queue around the Women's Building for "Lesbian Masquerade." Who passes for what? I'm sure some of the people lined up on 18th St were men masquerading as lesbians, passing, at least for that moment, as women, and hoping to find others like them, both living and dead. Others were undoubtedly there to cruise that line. I'd have belonged to both categories. Lou, not so much.

After the presentation Lou went up to Allan to talk about Babe Bean, a mysterious and attractive person who lived alone on a houseboat in the Sacramento Delta and refused to speak—not only about their manner of dress, but at all. Lou had found evidence that Babe Bean had started a new life as Jack Bee Garland.

> Saw Allan Bérubé again at his new lecture + he came to talk with me afterwards + I showed him my research. I said I felt guilty like I'm moving in on 'his' story, but he said emphatically, "Oh no! No!" Told him I'd phone him next wk + we could get together. He was pleased. Said I was the best person to do a book on him.[62]
> —Lou Sullivan, *We Both Laughed in Pleasure: The Selected Diaries of Lou Sullivan, 1961–1991*

Researcher to researcher, Lou asked Allan's permission to take over Jack Garland's biography, but Lou sidestepped those feminist arguments about who owns history that ultimately recast Allan's slideshow "Lesbian Masquerade" as the woman-made film *She Even Chewed Tobacco*, where I first met Babe Bean, who didn't care for the company of women and ran away to sea.

I gather each tidbit, each lead I pursue as tho I am finding someone
with whom I am in love. Jack Garland is my dad. The coroner's
report said he had cancer of the liver + spleen. When I first read it, I
thought it said she had iron-gray eyes, but today I looked closer and
it said brown eyes + iron gray hair. She had hair like an old man...
and I think of dad's beautiful white locks.

... (I like to call him "her" because it reminds me where I came
from and how lucky I am... how Jack Garland wanted to be Jack
Garland! I wonder if I'd've had the strength to live full-time as a man
before the luxury of hormones/surgery. I feel I want to have all the
surgery—to go all the way, in memory of Jack Garland.)[63]

In 1987 I saw *She Even Chewed Tobacco* and was secretly sad that Babe
Bean, the "Trouser Puzzle," wouldn't even talk to girls. In 1993, I read
From Female to Male and was disappointed that Jack Garland was only
interested in wholesome sailor boys. I didn't know yet what I might
become but I knew for sure that wasn't it. No wonder gay Lou imprinted
on Garland with such intense transcestral love; no wonder fag Zach
imprinted on Lou.

This is not a confession, it's a challenge.

> Frog fucking. Her hands on my hips; my heels against my ass, legs
> spread wide; her face leaning into my neck; my hands gripping
> her forearms. Her teeth are gentle. Nothing else about her is.
> I push up on the balls of my feet, rock my ass onto my ankles,
> reaching up for every forward movement of her thighs between
> mine. Her nipples are hard, her face flushed, feet planted on the
> floor while I arch off the edge of the bed, a water mammal, frog
> creature with thighs snapping back to meet her every thrust.[64]
> —**Dorothy Allison,** *Her Body, Mine, and His*

When E.G. invited me to dive into *OUT/LOOK* #11 she opened a portal to a time when I lived, amphibious, on the edge of several beds. Neither here nor there, neither fish nor fowl; there's a photograph of me sitting on a rock above the Golden Gate drinking wine out of the bottle, mohawk down and flowing in the wind off San Francisco Bay. Edward's blue scrawl on the back says *the nameless boy. 1991*

I was named for the 14th century English saint Julian of Norwich, who had visions of God as the Mother of all creation. She wrote them down in what is probably the first book written by a woman in English. Princes and bishops and common folk flocked to her. They hoped if they got close enough they, too, would experience the revelatory presence of a deity who kisses your boo-boo exactly where it hurts. Seven centuries later Julian is still revered for the visionary force of her writing. Wearing her name is a constant reminder that I am part of and can help to create a universe in which even God is as hermaphroditic as a snail. Like Radclyffe Hall's slim hips or Bill the Boilermaker's wad of chew, my name certifies my transness as innate, authentic, ineluctable.

But my name casts other things in doubt. To whom does it attach? My name-saint was herself nameless, known only by her address and her sex. Neither woman nor saint, I could not stay in Norwich.

For decades I called myself by other names. Then when I turned 50, I decided I was getting cluttered. I shed and pared away my previous selves until all that was left was a placeholder, the sign of incomplete presence, my first initial: simply, J. And for a year, that is what I was.

J. Bonnet died at the end of the line. Things didn't get better. The railroad shut down in 1910. After the second World War, redlining bankers gave Black people loans on the aging housing stock. In the 1950s, the I-280 freeway plowed through the resulting majority-Black community. In the 1960s the City "redeveloped" the historic Fillmore jazz district in central San Francisco, displacing another Black generation to the neighborhood then called Ocean View. Lost in a corner between two highways at the southern edge of the city, difficult to reach and easy for politicians to ignore, the area got poorer and poorer.

When I moved to San Francisco at the end of the 1980s it had a reputation as a bad, dangerous place riddled with bullets and crack. Nobody was putting up trans history plaques at the Chevron station on the barren intersection where McNamara's roadhouse had stood a century before. But in 1879, a person died there, a person who felt strongly enough about wearing trousers that they were willing to put up with the hassle of monthly arrests, a person who was getting into bed with a woman named Blanche, a person who made a decent living catching frogs to sell to restaurants, a person whose only recorded property at the time of death was a Colt pistol.

I washed my windshield, listening to the freeway overhead and considering driving over to Colma, where Bonnet's bones lie unsorted in a mass grave in what was called the Odd Fellows section, no lie. These days Bonnet's been claimed as a trancestor and the young ones call them Jean. I couldn't find any record of that name, but absence isn't meaningful evidence; the cops and the judges and the journalists were all invested in womaning this person who kept getting arrested for wearing men's clothes. At least once, Bonnet hired a lawyer who told the judge she had to wear pants because you can't catch frogs in a skirt. That much is true.

I wrote *Jean* on one side of a piece of paper, *Jeanne* on the other, and folded it into an origami frog. I hoped it would attract their ghostly attention. I wanted to open a channel so maybe I could tell them about the Chevron station and maybe they would tell me their truest name. Nothing much happened so I went back down to Oceanview and taped it to the back of the stop sign.

And in those days, in the city of New York, dwelt Lou Reed and his company, among them the woman Moe, who drummed. And their song went out into the land. In the city of Wisconsin that is called Milwaukee arose Sheila Sullivan, who heard the song of Lou, and took his name. In the 24th year of his life Lou journeyed to California. This is the book of the generations of Lou.

In San Francisco the tribe of the chroniclers were Jeffrey, and Allan, and Eric, and Greg, and Willie; and with them their sisters Amber and Estelle, and the butch called Gayle; these begat Susan. The tribe of the chroniclers walked in the Mission. Allan sang of the generations of Babe and of Jean. Babe begat Jack begat Lou. And Lou sang the song of his fathers.

Lou lived 30 years. Then a great plague come upon the land and many thousands died, and with them Lou who dwelt in San Francisco. The song of Lou passed from him to the children of the tribe of chroniclers: Susan who sang to open gender's gates, and her children and her children's children, and also those who guarded the portals.

These became the singers of the generations. And they walked in the Mission thirty years and more.

A few nights ago I texted Zach to ask whether he had any queer or trans association with the neighborhood around the Women's Building.

ZACH: *Yes! For one thing Lou wrote some Dolores Park journal entry but I have also gone on queer makeout dates / doesn't trans march meet there?*

ME: *Yup, in the part around 19th. Why were your makeout dates there?*

ZACH: *Other Julian probably suggested it—because of its queery transy aura probably*

ME: *Do you have a sense of a dyke past in that hood? I know you weren't one yourself but you certainly got fucked by them.*

ZACH: *Not to a names/dates level. Julian might, past life as butch-on-butch dyke. He's at the store, I'll ask when he comes home.*

ME: *Thx. I wonder if I woulda been too nelly for him . . .*

ZACH: *Ha ha maybe*

On 18th St outside the Women's Building, I walked back along the alley and pressed myself against its painted walls. I wanted to link up with J. Bonnet and the passing people in that line. Travelers we are, and makers of new ancestries, like at the moment when Allan spoke of Jack Garland and Lou felt a bone between his fingers. Amber stood beside Allan, and Jeffrey worked with them both as well as with E.G. on the *OUT/LOOK* project, and I met Gayle through Edward in a dungeon, and E.G. had slept with Amber back in Boston and connected her to me, and E.G. gave me the prompt that connected me to Zach so that I connected him back, through Susan, to Lou. (Sometimes I swear it feels like absolutely everything runs through Susan.)

ZACH: *The other thing to keep in mind is my queer experience of the bay was in Oakland not SF. I really didn't cross the bridge very much.*

ME: *Right but didn't you say history lives in conversation, especially between lovers?*
So if you had sex with people who connected to SF queer pasts it wouldn't be surprising if you had some shred of understanding through them, however vague

ZACH: *Yes true.*

I remember one when Lou's feeling the early effects of T sitting in the park in summer enjoying the sun warming his new arm hairs
He might also have kissed a guy after the pride march there
Julian says "is the Lex in that neighborhood?" Also a very queer friendly and racially mixed synagogue right by dolores
Sha'ar Zahav
We had a dyke-adjacent genderqueer friend w TransMan partner who lived near where the Lex used to be, and [trans lesbian ceramicist] Nicki Green lived nearby.
It's like we latch onto these spaces as queer spaces even though they aren't anymore and that makes them ours again.

We forge history with our feet. Approach and accompany,
advance and retreat. Hesitation, then
a bold rush forward:
Our lines keep curving around, back to where we started.
link hands, change partners,
link again.

A CLASP, CLOSING TO BEGIN

One of Susan's essays tells a story about how she and I sat on Bernal Hill, exchanging the memory pathways of our movement through the city, spread out below us in the sun. My leather daddy Edward taught me that classic San Francisco game around 1990, sitting on my tailgate up on Twin Peaks.

From that vantage point, you look out over the Castro and north Mission. You can see the length of the streets unreeling down the hill from Diamond Heights to the old bay shore: 14th crossing Market at Church where you could cruise the all-night Safeway after the gay AA meeting at the little cedar-shingled church across the street; 20th St, marking the uphill boundary of Dolores Park at the stretch we called Dolores Beach in honor of the almost-naked men spread out on the grass. Edward pointed out the vermilion block of the Construction Center by the freeway. In those days the building's manager lived illegally in a tiny box on the roof, smoking herb in a nest of live video monitors he'd built and connected himself, patrolling that vast lot from on high. I wonder where that manager's living now that it's so much harder to get away with breaking the rules about damn near everything, whether the past 20 years of gentrification swept him out of town like so many others. I wonder if he's still alive. He was shy and brown-eyed and the first man Edward kissed sober.

On the phone the other day I asked Edward when that fateful kiss took place. Early 1970s, he thought, but his memory for those kinds of facts began to fade when he turned 60, and that was a dozen years ago. I had a moment of aching for the details, lines of when and where, but truly these are less important than the experience
itself: the brush of two mustaches,
Edward so much
taller stooping holding
his breath: here we go.

The colons mark the way he paused when he said this to me all those years ago. A moment of reliving. Faithful: I held my breath when I recorded them. Whose story will it be when I begin to carry more of it than he does?

Increasingly I feel myself as a repository, a safe deposit, holding his memories for him as he puts them down.

Please read the kiss aloud like music so that your voice rises and suspends. Let my memory of his memory fill you. Hold your breath and mine and his as elements of our collective queer trans/sexuality, many generations' experience, many moments of desire and transformation condensed into this tiny story expanding your lungs, entering your bloodstream, rushing through your channels.

Then relax. Soften your portals.
Send the kiss back out into the sky.

ENDNOTES

1. E.G. Crichton, *Matchmaking in the Archive: 19 Conversations with the Dead and 3 Encounters with Ghosts* (New Brunswick, NJ: Rutgers University Press, 2023), 183.

2. Eliza Steinbock, *Shimmering Images: Trans Cinema, Embodiment, and the Aesthetics of Change* (Durham, NC: Duke University Press, 2019).

3. Lou Sullivan, *We Both Laughed in Pleasure: The Selected Diaries of Lou Sullivan, 1961–1991*, ed. Ellis Martin and Zach Ozma (New York: Nightboat Books, 2019), 402.

4. Karen Barad, "Transmaterialities: Trans*/Matter/Realities and Queer Political Imaginings," *GLQ: A Journal of Lesbian and Gay Studies* 21, no. 2–3 (June 2015): 408.

5. Louis de Jaucourt, "Skin, pores of the," in *The Encyclopedia of Diderot & d'Alembert Collaborative Translation Project*, trans. Audra Merfeld-Langston and Kelly Dunlap (Ann Arbor: Michigan Publishing, University of Michigan Library, 2015), http://hdl.handle.net/2027/spo.did2222.0003.141. Originally published as "Peau, pores de la," in *Encyclopédie ou Dictionnaire raisonné des sciences, des arts et des métiers*, 12:215 (N.p.: Paris, 1765).

6. Peter Godfrey-Smith, *Metazoa: Animal Minds and the Birth of Consciousness* (London: Harper Collins, 2020), 30.

7. Godfrey-Smith, 30.

8. Godfrey-Smith, 31.

9. Godfrey-Smith, 31.

10. Godfrey-Smith, 31.

11. Barad, "TransMaterialities," 408.

12. Samuel Delany, *The Motion of Light in Water: Sex and Science Fiction Writing in the East Village* (New York: Arbor House: 1988), 20.

13. William Pope.L, interview by Martha Wilson, *BOMB Magazine* #55, April 1996, https://bombmagazine.org/articles/william-pope-l

14. Pope.L, interview.

15. Pope.L, interview.

16. Barad, "TransMaterialities," 397.

17. Sara Ahmed, *Strange Encounters: Embodied Others in Post-Coloniality* (New Brunswick, NJ: Rutgers University Press, 2000), 48.

18. Judith Butler, *Undoing Gender* (New York: Routledge, 2004), 23.

19. *Oxford English Dictionary*, s.v. "Enchain," last modified December 2022, https://www.oed.com/view/Entry/61648.

20. "History of Anchor Design," Anchors R Us, accessed June 21, 2022, http://anchors.synthasite.com/history-1.php.

21. John H. Harland, "The Transition from Hemp to Chain Cable: Innovations and Innovators," *The Mariner's Mirror* 99, no. 1 (2013): 72, https://www.tandfonline.com/doi/full/10.1080/00253359.2013.767000.

22. Harland, 74.

23. https://www.nytimes.com/2020/04/09/science/neanderthals-fiber-string-math.html.

24. John Robb and Oliver J. T. Harris, "Becoming Gendered in European Prehistory: Was Neolithic Gender Fundamentally Different?" *American Antiquity* 83, no. 1 (2018): 134, 136.

25. J.R. Stark and J.R. Smith, *Classical Loop-in-Loop Chains and their Derivatives* (Boston: Springer, 1997), 2.

26. Sullivan, *We Both Laughed in Pleasure*, 81.

27. Betty Nelson Curryer, *Anchors: An Illustrated History* (Annapolis, MD: Naval Institute, 1999), 104.

28. "Chains and Their Manufacture," *THE IRON AGE* LXX (July 3, 1902): 6.

29. Melissa J. Homestead, *American Women Authors and Literary Property, 1822–1869* (New York: Cambridge University Press, 2005), 29.

30. Fred Wilson, "Metalwork, 1793–1880" from exhibition *Mining the Museum* (1992–1993), Maryland Center for History and Culture, accessed June 21, 2023, https://www.mdhistory.org/resources/mining-the-museum-metalwork-1793-1880/.

31. Judy Grahn, Untitled ("In the place where"), in *Edward the Dyke and Other Poems* (Oakland, CA: The Women's Press Collective, 1971).

32. David J. Getsy, *Queer Behavior: Scott Burton and Performance Art* (Chicago: University of Chicago Press, 2022). David, I apologize for the reductive summary. Prosody made me do it.

33. Julian Thomas, "Death, Identity and the Body in Neolithic Britain," *The Journal of the Royal Anthropological Institute* 6, no. 4 (December 2000): 659.

34. Thomas, 659.

35. Thomas, 659.

36. Michel Foucault, "Nietzsche, Genealogy, History," in *The Foucault Reader*, ed. Paul Rabinow (New York: Pantheon Books, 1984), 95.

37. Sarah Schulman, *Let the Record Show: A Political History of ACT UP New York, 1987–1993* (New York: Farrar, Strauss, Giroux, 2021), 5.

38. David Wojnarowicz, *Close to the Knives: A Memoir of Disintegration* (New York: Vintage Books, 1991), 105–106.

39. Douglas Crimp, "Mourning and Militancy," *October* 51 (Winter 1989): 11.

40. Hollie Clark et al., "Diagnosed HIV infection in Transgender Adults and Adolescents: Results from the National HIV Surveillance System, 2009–2014," *AIDS and Behavior* 21 (2017): 2774–83, https://doi.org/10.1007/s10461-016-1656-7.

41. "Jon Greenberg Speech for Mark Lowe Fisher's Funeral," as delivered by Barbara Hughes at Greenberg's political funeral in Tompkins Square Park, New York, July 16, 1993, https://actupny.org/diva/polfunsyn.html#speech.

42. Susan Stryker, "My Words to Victor Frankenstein Above the Village of Chamounix," *Transgender Studies Reader* Vol. 2, ed. Susan Stryker and Aren Z. Azura (New York: Routledge, 2013), 249.

43. Dan Guillory, "The Dilemma of Dickson Mounds," *Illinois Issues* XIV, no. 12 (December 1990): 21–25.

44. There's a large body of scholarship exploring the cultural history of the imaginary Native American; the work that founded the field is Philip J.

Deloria, *Playing Indian* (New Haven: Yale University Press, 1999). For a recent visual exploration see contemporary multimedia artist Canuppa Hanska Luger, especially *Regalia* (2013-2014.), a series of sculptures that reflects on contemporary fashion's (mis)use of indigenous adornment. https://www.cannupahanska.com/

45. Cynthia Carr, *Fire in the Belly: The Life and Times of David Wojnarowicz* (New York: Bloomsbury USA, 2012), 431.

46. Laura Lawless, *Lawless French*, s.v. "Enchainement/Liaison," accessed June 21, 2022, https://www.lawlessfrench.com/pronunciation/enchainement.

47. Elizabeth Kennedy and Madeline Davis, *Boots of Leather, Slippers of Gold: The History of a Lesbian Community* (New York: Routledge, 1993).

48. *Bowers v. Hardwick*, 478 U.S. 186 (1986).

49. Judy Grahn, (N.p.: n.p., 1972).

50. *Felton v. State*, S07A1439 (GA.2008), https://caselaw.findlaw.com/ga-supreme-court/1475463.html.

51. Jennifer Lawrence, "Temps," *Artistry House Productions* (blog), March 31, 2017, https://www.artistryhouseproductions.com/ballet-terminology-blog/2017/3/26/temps-temps-lev-temps-de-cuisse-contretemps.

52. Xandra Ibarra, "The Hookup/Displacement/Barhopping/Drama Tour," accessed June 21, 2023, http://www.xandraibarra.com/the-makeoutdisplacementbarhoppingdrama-tour.

53. Bruce Nauman, *Body Pressure*, 1974, offset lithograph, 25 x 16½" (64 x 42 cm).

54. T Fleischmann, *Time is the Thing a Body Moves Through* (Minneapolis: Coffee House, 2021), 7.

55. Sullivan, *We Both Laughed in Pleasure*, 13.

56. The San Francisco Gay and Lesbian History Project [Allan Bérubé, Jeffrey Escoffier, Amber Hollibaugh, Willie Walker], interview by Terrence Kissick and Molly McGarry, October 10, 1995, New York, conducted for the Radical History Review. Transcript in author's possession, gift of Jeffrey Escoffier.

57. *"She Even Chewed Tobacco": She Drank, She Swore, She Even Courted Girls: Passing Women in 19th Century America*, directed by Elizabeth Stevens and Estelle Freedman (New York: Women Make Movies, 1983), https://www.moviefone.com/movie/she-even-chewed-tobacco/e2fFl1gEvg3G5EnLuuhdh/main.

58. San Francisco Lesbian and Gay History Project, "*She Even Chewed Tobacco*: A Pictorial Narrative," in *Hidden from History: Reclaiming the Lesbian and Gay Past*, ed. Martin Duberman, Martha Vicinus, and George Chauncey, Jr. (New York: Penguin Books, 1989), 183–184.

59. Havelock Ellis, "Sexual Inversion," in *Studies in the Psychology of Sex* Vol. 2, 3rd ed. (Philadelphia: F.A. Davis, 1921), 249.

60. Radclyffe Hall, *The Well of Loneliness* (London: Jonathan Cape, 1928; London: Penguin Books, 2015), 483–84.

61. San Francisco Lesbian and Gay History Project interview, 10.

62. Sullivan, *We Both Laughed in Pleasure*, 331.

63. Sullivan, *We Both Laughed in Pleasure*, 331, 337.

64. Dorothy Allison, "Her Body, Mine, and His," in *Leatherfolk*, ed. Mark Thompson (Boston: Alyson Publications, 1991), 44.

Acknowledgments

I am deeply indebted to the writers, artists, activists, and perverts whose work has shaped our common world. I'm especially grateful to E.G. Crichton, the late Jeffrey Escoffier, and all who pioneered the practices of love currently manifesting as the San Francisco GLBT Historical Society Museum and Archives. I hope I've made my ancestors both chuckle and cry.

My mother's death during the writing process saved us from some excruciating conversations, but I like to think she'd have enjoyed the music of my language and my reliance on the *OED*. Thank you, Mama, for teaching me how to read.

Julian Carter has been thinking with his body for a very long time. Both his scholarship and his creative practice examine pleasure, power, and the bodily ways of being through which people experience self and community belonging. He is the author of *The Heart of Whiteness: Normal Sexuality and Race in America, 1890-1940*, and has published in numerous journals and anthologies, including *GLQ; TSQ: Trans Studies Quarterly; TDR: The Drama Review; The Journal of the History of Sexuality; The Transgender Studies Reader Vol. 2; The Transgender Studies Remix; Queer Dance: Makings and Meanings; About Face: Stonewall, Revolt, and the New Queer Art*; and the *Routledge Companion to Queer Art History*. Carter is Associate Professor of Critical Studies and Fine Arts at the California College of the Arts in San Francisco. He also dances, draws, and instigates creative interventions in conventional academic contexts.

NIGHTBOAT BOOKS

Nightboat Books, a nonprofit organization, seeks to develop audiences for writers whose work resists convention and transcends boundaries. We publish books rich with poignancy, intelligence, and risk. Please visit nightboat.org to learn about our titles and how you can support our future publications.

The following individuals have supported the publication of this book. We thank them for their generosity and commitment to the mission of Nightboat Books:

Kazim Ali, Anonymous (8), Mary Armantrout, Jean C. Ballantyne, Thomas Ballantyne, Bill Bruns, John Cappetta, V. Shannon Clyne, Ulla Dydo Charitable Fund, Photios Giovanis, Amanda Greenberger, Vandana Khanna, Isaac Klausner, Shari Leinwand, Anne Marie Macari, Elizabeth Madans, Martha Melvoin, Caren Motika, Elizabeth Motika, The Leslie Scalapino - O Books Fund, Robin Shanus, Thomas Shardlow, Rebecca Shea, Ira Silverberg, Benjamin Taylor, David Wall, Jerrie Whitfield & Richard Motika, Arden Wohl, Issam Zineh

This book is made possible, in part, by grants from the New York City Department of Cultural Affairs in partnership with the City Council and the New York State Council on the Arts Literature Program.